Richard M. Nixon

37th President of
the United States

Perhaps no other American President has been the center of as much controversy as Richard Milhous Nixon, the only President to resign from office before his term ended. The real achievements of his administration were overshadowed by the Watergate scandal, which caused his downfall. (Nixon Project, National Archives.)

Richard M. Nixon

37th President of the United States

Rebecca Stefoff

GARRETT EDUCATIONAL CORPORATION

Cover: *Official presidential portrait of Richard M. Nixon by J. Anthony Wills.* (Copyrighted by the White House Historical Association; photograph by the National Geographic Society.)

Manufactured in the United States of America

Edited and produced by Synthegraphics Corporation

Library of Congress Cataloging in Publication Data

Stefoff, Rebecca, 1951–
  Richard M. Nixon, 37th President of the United States / Rebecca Stefoff.
    p.   cm. – (Presidents of the United States)
  Includes bibliographical references.
  Summary: Presents the life of Richard M. Nixon, including his childhood, education, employment, and political career.
  1. Nixon, Richard M. (Richard Milhous), 1913–
–Juvenile literature.   2. Presidents–United States–
Biography–Juvenile literature.   3. United States–
Politics and government–1969–1974–Juvenile literature.   [1. Nixon, Richard M. (Richard Milhous), 1913–   .   2. Presidents.]   I. Title.   II. Series.
E856.S74   1990
973.924′092–dc20
[B]
[92]   88-39944
ISBN 0-944483-59-3   CIP
                                                  AC

Contents

Chronology for
Richard M. Nixon

1913 Born on January 9 in Yorba Linda, California

1930– Attended Whittier College
1934

1937 Graduated from Duke University Law School

1940 Married Thelma Catherine ("Pat") Ryan on June 21

1942– Served in U.S. Navy during World War II
1945

1946 Elected to the U.S. House of Representatives

1950 Elected to the U.S. Senate

1952 Elected Vice-President under President Dwight D. Eisenhower; re-elected in 1956

1960 Lost presidential election to John F. Kennedy

1962 Lost election for governorship of California

1968 Elected 37th President of the United States

1972 Re-elected President

1974 Resigned as President on August 9; retired to California and later to New York and then New Jersey

Chapter 1

The Fall from Power

On a hot July day in 1974, with an overcast sky threatening thunder and rain over Washington, D.C., eight of the nine justices of the United States Supreme Court solemnly took their seats in the stately square hall of the nation's most important courtroom. In the crowded visitors' galleries, reporters held pencils poised over their notepads, ready to break the biggest news story in the land. The Supreme Court chamber had witnessed many landmarks in U.S. history, but none more dramatic than this occasion. The eight men were about to announce their judgment in a case that pitted the United States of America against Richard M. Nixon, its President.

EXECUTIVE PRIVILEGE

The case concerned something called "executive privilege." This is the term used to describe the right of the President, as the country's chief executive, to protect the secrecy of information that might be important to national security. Executive privilege had been established over many previous presidential administrations. Presidents have argued that the government could not function well if certain kinds of information—military plans, for example, or campaign strategies, or "deals" between politicians—were made public. Now the Supreme Court was forced to decide just how far the President could go in keeping information from the public in order to protect himself.

The information in question was a series of tape recordings. Nixon had installed an elaborate, secret system of microphones and tape recorders in the White House to record almost all of his activities there, including conversations with his assistants and advisors. In the summer of 1974, some of those advisors were on trial for criminal offenses connected with their jobs for the President, and the recordings contained evidence that could prove them guilty or innocent. And although President Nixon himself was not on trial, everyone knew that the secret tapes also contained the truth about his own guilt or innocence in a variety of illegal acts and maneuvers. The U.S. Congress had ordered the President to release the tapes. Nixon had refused. Both had appealed to the Supreme Court to settle the matter, and the nation waited tensely for the outcome.

Chief Justice Warren Burger, who had been appointed to the Supreme Court by Nixon five years earlier, spoke for the Court. Although executive privilege does and should exist, he said, it is the Supreme Court's duty to decide how that privilege is limited by the law. He added that executive privilege must give way to the need for evidence in a criminal trial. In short, the Court upheld Congress' demand for the tapes. The gavel thudded, the justices filed silently out of the chamber through a door in the wine-colored velvet wall hangings, and the case was closed. The President had lost.

A LONG, LOSING BATTLE

The Supreme Court judgment was one of the final episodes in a long series of scandals that history remembers as "the Watergate affair." For two years, ever since a handful of men were arrested for breaking into an office in the Watergate building in Washington, D.C., on June 17, 1972, President Nixon had fought to keep the public from finding out about certain things that he and his supporters in the White House and in the Republican Party had done to preserve their power.

The Watergate break-in was a typical example of these activities. It was a bungled attempt to plant an illegal listening device, or "bug," in the headquarters of the Democratic Party to spy on the Democrats' campaign plans for the November 1972 presidential election. Accounts of the break-in appeared in the nation's newspapers the day after it happened, but the incident seemed unimportant at the time—even a little silly. Nor did it damage Nixon's prestige at first. Everyone just assumed that a few overly eager supporters of the President had acted foolishly and without his knowledge.

Five months later, in November 1972, Nixon was re-elected to a second term as President by a large majority of American voters. But as the months passed, investigators from both newspapers and the government discovered that the Watergate break-in was like the tip of an iceberg. Bit by bit during 1973 and the early months of 1974, a deeply disturbing picture emerged. It seemed that members of the Nixon administration had been involved in illegal wiretapping and other forms of spying on private citizens, in accepting illegal campaign contributions, in failing to pay income taxes, in bribery, in perjury (the crime of lying under oath in a court of law), and in burglaries.

As soon as the Watergate break-in occurred, Nixon and his assistants tried to "cover up," or conceal, the administration's involvement. But the cover-up failed, and soon Americans began asking some urgent questions: Did the President authorize the break-in? If not, when did he find out about it? Did he order his assistants to lie about it? Did he lie about it? And what was going on in the Nixon White House, anyway?

The Threat of Impeachment

For two bitter years, President Nixon fought a losing battle against the reporters who covered the Watergate case and the congressmen and attorneys who investigated it. Then, when he was accused both of not paying his income taxes and also of interfering with the Watergate investigation, he made a direct appeal to the American public. On nationwide television, he announced, "In all my years of public life I have never obstructed justice. . . . I welcome this kind of examination because people have got to know whether or not their President is a crook. Well," he concluded angrily, "I am not a crook." But many viewers were troubled and embarrassed that their President felt the need to speak of himself in such terms. The speech did not win any support for Nixon.

For a while, Nixon gained time by refusing to cooperate with the investigators, but in July 1974, when the Supreme Court ordered him to hand over his tape-recorded conversations, that time ran out. The tapes that Nixon was ordered to surrender contained unmistakable evidence in the President's own voice and words that he had known about the Watergate cover-up.

Furthermore, not only had Nixon known that his supporters were lying to investigators from the Justice Department, he had actually instructed them to lie. During the cover-up attempt, he had even tried to use the Central Intelligence Agency (CIA), the nation's international espionage force, to interfere with the law-enforcement activities of the Federal Bureau of Investigation (FBI). But in obstructing justice in this way, Nixon had broken the law of the land. As a lawbreaker, he could be impeached—that is, charged with crimes by the House of Representatives to stand trial before the Senate. Only one other President had ever been impeached: Andrew Johnson, in 1868. Johnson was acquitted

Opposition to Nixon grew as details of the Watergate affair became public. At an anti-Nixon rally in front of the White House in October 1973, one protestor wore a Nixon mask and a jailbird suit. (Copyright *Washington Post;* reprinted by permission of the D.C. Public Library.)

by the Senate, but most observers in 1974 felt that Nixon would not be so lucky.

A Violation of Trust

Above and beyond the specific crimes with which he could be charged, Nixon was guilty of violating the trust placed in him by the voters. Many people believed that he had used the powers of his office for personal political benefits and not necessarily in the best interests of the nation. To these people, Nixon had disgraced the presidency and the American system of democratic government.

By the summer of 1974, even Nixon's closest friends and supporters had to admit that he stood little chance of surviving an impeachment. In the final days of July and the first days of August, one by one they reluctantly advised him to do what no other American President had ever done before: to resign.

FAREWELL TO OFFICE

On August 8, just two weeks after the Supreme Court hearing on the White House tapes, crowds lined several blocks of Pennsylvania Avenue in the nation's capital. Some of the people who had been waiting for more than a day sat on blankets or park benches; others paced up and down, gazing across a wrought-iron fence and a wide green lawn to the White House. The mood was quiet, without anger, violence, or jubilation. The feeling of history-making was in the air as lights glowed in the President's Oval Office.

That evening, in a nationwide television address from his office, Richard M. Nixon became the first U.S. President to give up his high office:

> I have never been a quitter. To leave office before my term is completed is abhorrent to every instinct in my body. But as President, I must put the interest of America first. America needs a full-time President and a full-time Congress, particularly at this time with the problems we face at home and abroad.
>
> To continue to fight through the months ahead for my personal vindication would almost totally absorb the time and attention of both the President and the Congress in a period when our entire focus should be on the great issues of peace abroad and prosperity without inflation at home.
>
> Therefore, I shall resign the Presidency effective at noon tomorrow. Vice-President Ford will be sworn in as President at that hour in this office.

Nixon then went on to speak of the high hopes with which he had begun his second term and of his regret that he would not be able to fulfill all of those hopes. Referring to the conflicts and divisions that had shaken the nation in the preceding few years, he said that he hoped his resignation would hasten "the start of that process of healing which is so desperately needed in America." His only reference to the Watergate scandal that had brought about his downfall was an indirect one. He did not mention Watergate or the charges that had been made against him and his supporters, but he said, "I regret deeply any injuries that may have been done in the course of the events that led to this decision. I would say only that if some of my judgments were wrong, and some were wrong, they were made in what I believed at that time to be in the best interest of the nation."

Then, after reflecting briefly on the successes for which

With his daughter Tricia and his son-in-law Edward Cox at his side, Nixon makes his farewell speech in front of the television cameras. (Nixon Project, National Archives.)

he hoped to be remembered, Nixon ended his farewell to the nation with these words: "To have served in this office is to have felt a very personal sense of kinship with each and every American. In leaving it, I do so with this prayer: May God's grace be with you in all the days ahead."

On the following day, Nixon waited until Vice-President Gerald Ford had been sworn in as President. Then, after a tearful farewell to the staff of servants, attendants, and assistants that had served him and his family for more than five years, he left the White House.

Richard M. Nixon had devoted his life to winning the presidency. He had fought hard and worked endlessly to reach his goal, and he had experienced brutal defeats and humiliations as well as triumphs on the way to the Oval Office. Now he had lost it all, in the biggest humiliation of his lifetime — and the bitterest defeat any U.S. President had ever faced. Silently, proud even in defeat, he returned to his home state, California, where the Richard Nixon story had begun 61 years before.

Chapter 2
California Roots

Unlike such Presidents as John F. Kennedy, Franklin D. Roosevelt, and Theodore Roosevelt, Richard Nixon did not come from an upper-class or wealthy family with a tradition of leadership. His background is more like that of Presidents Abraham Lincoln and Andrew Jackson: a humble, working-class family with little money. Like Lincoln and Jackson, Nixon was a self-made man with very ordinary roots.

FATHER'S HERITAGE

On his father's side, Nixon is descended from Scottish and Irish ancestors. The first of his father's ancestors to arrive in the American colonies was James Nixon, who settled in Delaware in 1753. Two of James' sons fought in the American Revolution; one of them, George, was among the soldiers who crossed the Delaware River with General George Washington in 1776.

After the Revolution, George Nixon and his brother moved westward, into the American frontier along the Ohio

River. Two generations later, President Nixon's great-grandfather, George Nixon III, enlisted in an Ohio Regiment during the Civil War. He was killed at the Battle of Gettysburg. One of George's sons, Samuel Brady Nixon, had a son of his own in 1878 in Vinton County, Ohio. This boy, Francis Anthony Nixon (always called Frank) was President Nixon's father.

Frank Nixon's mother died when he was young, and his father had to work hard at several jobs to keep the family from poverty. Frank's childhood became even more unhappy when his father remarried, because Frank and his stepmother disliked one another.

At 14, after just managing to pass the fourth grade in school, Frank decided that neither more schooling nor the life of a farmer appealed to him. He ran away from home and took up the first of a long series of jobs.

As a young man, Frank Nixon was a Democrat, but a chance encounter in 1896 changed that. Republican William McKinley came to town and, during a parade, complimented Frank on his handsome horse. From that time on, Frank was a Republican. His strong support of the Republican Party later shaped young Richard Nixon's political thinking.

In 1907, after suffering frostbitten toes that became painful in the cold Ohio winters, Frank moved west to California. He found work on a ranch near the small town of Whittier, outside of Los Angeles. It was in Whittier that he met and married Hannah Milhous.

MOTHER'S HERITAGE

Hannah Milhous' ancestors were originally from Germany, although the family claims a distant connection to King Edward III of England (1312–1377). The family moved to Ireland in the 17th century, and there they became members of William Penn's new church, the Society of Friends, or Quakers as they were called. In 1729 Thomas Milhous brought his family across the ocean to Pennsylvania. By the early 1800s, Milhouses were living in Ohio, and in 1854 they settled in Indiana. Richard Nixon's maternal grandfather, Franklin Milhous, was then six years old. Like many Quaker families, the Milhouses were opposed to slavery, and their home was a station on the Underground Railroad for escaped slaves.

Franklin Milhous later married and had nine children, including a daughter named Hannah, who was born in 1885. The Milhouses were quiet, thrifty, hardworking Quakers who believed strongly in education, honesty, and family life. They were staunch Republicans, too. Franklin's wife, Almira, who was Richard Nixon's grandmother, "virtually worshipped Lincoln," Richard later recalled.

In the 1880s, Franklin Milhous became interested in the idea of moving to California. Like many Americans, he was attracted by accounts of the mild weather and fruitful soil of the West Coast. Quakers found California particularly appealing after 1887, when the Society of Friends founded a new Quaker community there called Whittier, after John Greenleaf Whittier, a well-known Quaker poet. So many members of the Society moved west to live in Whittier that the town soon became the largest Quaker community in the United States. In 1897, Franklin Milhous joined this westward flow. He prospered in California, first cultivating an orange grove and later dealing in real estate.

FRANK AND HANNAH

Hannah Milhous attended Whittier College for two years and then became a schoolteacher. She was slim, dark-eyed, and serious. In 1908 she met a well-dressed, talkative young man

A Quaker in the White House

The Society of Friends, as the Quaker church is formally known, was founded in England in 1652 by George Fox. But the Church of England was not tolerant of the new religion, and many Quakers were imprisoned or fined. Within a few years, Quakers who were fleeing such persecution had brought their religion to the American colonies. The most famous American Quaker was William Penn, who had joined the Society of Friends in 1666. He founded the Quaker colony of Pennsylvania in 1681 as a ''holy experiment'' in religious life. Penn and other Pennsylvania Quakers had friendlier, more peaceful relations with the Indians than did any other group of American colonists.

During the 19th century, American Quakers played an important role in the antislavery movement. Many of them were abolitionists, like Nixon's Milhous ancestors, who supported the Underground Railroad. A number of them fought in the Civil War because of their antislavery beliefs, although the Quaker religion forbids any type of fighting or military service.

Today there are about 250,000 members of the Society of Friends around the world. Some 125,000 of these are in the United States and Canada, and the rest are in Europe, Latin America, and Africa. Friends churches and service groups are noted for their charitable work around the world. In 1947 Friends service groups won the Nobel

Peace Prize for their aid to refugees during World War II.

Richard Nixon was not the first Quaker President of the United States. Herbert Hoover, a distant cousin of Nixon who was President from 1929 to 1933, came from a long line of American Quaker ancestors. Because the Quaker faith forbids its members to swear oaths, Hoover changed the wording of the oath of office when he was sworn in as President. Instead of "I do solemnly swear," he said, "I do solemnly affirm." Nixon, however, does not seem to have taken his religion as seriously after his college years, for he did not change the wording of the oath.

at a Valentine's Day dance at the Friends Church in East Whittier. The young man was Frank Nixon, who had become a Quaker and joined the church soon after arriving in Whittier—because, some say, he found that there was no social life in the community for anyone who was not a Quaker. At any rate, Frank and Hannah began seeing each other and soon fell in love.

Some members of the Milhous family felt that a common laborer such as Frank, and one who had not been raised a Quaker, was not a good enough match for Hannah. But Hannah spiritedly disagreed, and she had her way. The two were married four months after they met. The marriage was a happy and successful one, although the newlyweds were to endure their share of sorrow and hard times.

Nixon was born in this house in Yorba Linda, California, in 1913. His father had built the house one year earlier. (Library of Congress.)

Early Years

For a few years after their marriage, Frank and Hannah Nixon lived in homes owned by Hannah's father while Frank worked on Milhous ranches. Their first child, a boy they named Harold, was born in 1909. Then, in 1912, Franklin Milhous loaned the young family money to buy a lemon grove in a tiny town called Yorba Linda. Frank Nixon built a wooden frame house there, worked hard in the grove (which was never very successful), and taught Sunday school at a Quaker church.

On January 9, 1913, the couple's second child was born—

a plump, loud-voiced boy whom his parents named Richard (for King Richard the Lion-Hearted) Milhous Nixon. A neighbor later remembered that Frank Nixon threw his hands into the air with delight and danced around his yard, crying, "I've got another boy!" Eventually, Frank and Hannah would have three more sons: Donald, born in 1914; Arthur, born in 1918; and Edward, born in 1930.

The Nixons lived in Yorba Linda until 1922. During Richard's childhood there, the family was always on the edge of poverty. The lemon grove was unfruitful, and there was little money for anything beyond food and clothing for the growing family. The Nixons never ate in a restaurant or took even a brief vacation.

As a small child, Richard had little understanding of his parents' financial struggles. His early life was one of boyish stubbornness. He swam in the dangerous Anaheim Canal in spite of repeated warnings from his father, and he insisted upon standing up to ride in the family wagon, although once a fall gave him a serious head injury. He displayed a competitive streak at an early age and would never turn down a challenge or a dare. He also loved to be read to, and after age five he could read on his own. *National Geographic* was his favorite magazine.

The only toy the Nixon boys owned was a small train set. Richard loved to pretend he was the engineer, and years later he recalled lying in bed at night, reading and listening to the whistle of the trains on a nearby railroad, which always made him daydream about visiting faraway places. He called the train whistle "the sweetest music I ever heard." His goal was to be an engineer when he grew up.

Life in the Nixon household was not easy. In addition to the family's money problems, Frank Nixon's personality created some stress for his sons. He was a stern parent, and misbehavior was punished with a strap. He also loved to ar-

A portrait of the Nixon family shows Frank and Hannah with their three oldest sons (left to right): Harold, Donald, and Richard. (Copyright *Washington Post;* reprinted by permission of the D.C. Public Library.)

gue, state his opinions, and even shout. Neighbors and relatives long remembered the "tempestuous arguments" between Frank and Harold that could be heard all over the neighborhood.

Richard's mother, on the other hand, never punished her sons; instead, she would have long, emotional discussions with them whenever they had done wrong (Nixon later said, "In our family, we would always prefer spanking"). She was patient with Frank's terrible temper and his argumentative ways. She also shared with Richard her love of music, and he became a good performer on the piano and the violin.

In some areas, Richard's parents agreed: they both believed in the value of education and hard work, and they both tried hard to give their sons pride in themselves and the feeling that they could be successful. "There was a drive to succeed," the President later said of his early years.

Back to Whittier

In 1922, when Richard was nine years old, Frank Nixon finally admitted defeat with the lemon grove. He sold the Yorba Linda property and took his family back to Whittier, where oil had recently been discovered. At first he worked in the oil fields. Later he operated a gas station and then a small grocery store called Nixon's Market. Everyone in the family worked in the store. Richard did everything from mashing potatoes to sweeping the floor. When he was old enough to drive, he was given the job of trucking produce from Los Angeles to the store every morning before school. He would get up at 4 A.M., drive to the farmers' market in Los Angeles, pick up a load of fruit and vegetables, and return to Whittier, where he would clean and arrange the produce in the store. Then he would go to school.

From his first year in school, Richard was an excellent and hardworking student. He brought home A's and was the best student in his school at memorizing and reciting poetry or passages from textbooks. His gift of memory never deserted him. As a child, he read Mark Twain's *Tom Sawyer* many times; he especially loved the scene where Tom tricked his friends into painting the fence for him. Many years later, when Nixon was President, one of Twain's descendants visited him in the White House. Nixon recited the entire fence-painting scene from the book without a mistake for his astonished guest.

A Love for Debating

Richard also gained a reputation as a debater. Even before high school, he loved to read newspapers and discuss issues. He took an interest in politics, which was surprising in so young a boy. He was ten years old when a scandal called the "Teapot Dome Affair" blackened the reputation of President Warren G. Harding. It is reported that he looked up from a newspaper account of the affair and said gravely to his mother, "I would like to become an honest lawyer, one who can't be bought by crooks."

In high school, Richard's interest in debating increased, as did his skill. This type of formal, structured argument appealed to his logical mind and gave his serious personality a chance to shine. He won several debating contests and spent whatever spare time he could find listening to the debate teams of other schools. His success as a debater would be reflected in his later career in law and politics, where his speechmaking skills were a great help.

Richard Nixon threw himself into high school with the

same intense energy that he applied to everything else he did. He played violin in the orchestra, he worked on the school newspaper, and he joined the Latin club. In addition to these scholarly pursuits, he tried endlessly to succeed at sports. He tried out for the football, basketball, and track teams. Although he showed up for every practice and did his best, he never made a starting team.

Another area in which Richard struggled during his high school years was in personal relationships. Although he socialized with his cousin, Merle West, and a few other young men, he did not seem to have any truly close friends. He did run for president of his senior class but was defeated by one of the school's best-liked athletes. Richard was shy and awkward with most of the girls he knew, although midway through his senior year he began dating a popular and attractive girl named Ola Florence Welsh.

Family Milestones

The years after the family's return to Whittier brought more than study and work to Richard. They also included some personal milestones, both tragic and happy. The biggest tragedy of his early life occurred in 1925, when his beloved younger brother Arthur died of tuberculosis. Hannah Nixon said that after Arthur's death, the 12-year-old Richard "sank into a deep, impenetrable silence." Nixon himself said, "For weeks after Arthur's funeral there was not a day that I did not think of him and cry."

Several years later, Richard's older brother Harold also became ill with tuberculosis. The family tried everything to keep Harold alive, including selling some land in order to pay for nursing care and for a stay at an expensive private hospital in Arizona. When the money ran out, Hannah insisted that Harold needed the Arizona mountain air, so she paid for a cottage there by taking care of three other tubercular patients. During two summer vacations, Richard managed to find part-time jobs in Arizona when he went there to visit his brother and his mother.

All of Hannah Nixon's care and Frank Nixon's sacrifices could not save Harold. He died in 1933, when Richard was 20 years old. Richard had loved his open-hearted, popular brother, and he felt not only grief but loneliness after Harold's death. In the meantime, however, a family event of a different kind had occurred when Richard was 17 and in his senior year at Whittier High School. The fifth and final child of Frank and Hannah Nixon was born in 1930. He was named Edward.

WHITTIER COLLEGE

Richard graduated from high school in 1930. He possessed extraordinary intelligence and ambition, but his ambitious nature received a serious setback that year. He graduated first in his class and won his high school's Harvard Club award as "best all-around student." The award was a scholarship to Harvard University in Cambridge, Massachusetts. In addition, he seemed likely to win a scholarship to Yale University in New Haven, Connecticut. Nixon had dreamed for years of going to a famous college "back East," but his dreams were shattered when he had to turn down both opportunities. Because Harold's long illness had drained the family's funds, there was no money to pay for the cost of traveling to the East Coast and living there. Richard swallowed his disappointment and enrolled at Whittier College.

Whittier was a college of about 400 students. It had been founded in 1887 as a Quaker school, but by 1930 it was open to students of all faiths. The college was still strongly religious, however. All students were required to attend chapel three times a week, and smoking and dancing were forbidden on campus.

A College Spokesman

Richard approached college in the same energetic way that he had gone to high school. He played on the football team and devoted an enormous amount of time and energy to practice, although he never was anything but a minor player. His love of debate also stayed with him, and he became captain of the college debating team.

One of Richard's activities as a debater was especially important in preparing him for his later political life. He became a student spokesman for the college and appeared before many businessmen's clubs, church groups, and community organizations to boost the school. This experience helped him become accustomed to meeting groups and making a good impression on them. When he started his political career a few years later, he began by speaking in front of those same church and business organizations.

During college, Richard also joined the singing club and the drama club. He appeared in several plays; in fact, he had the starring role in the school play during his junior year. In high school he had been a stiff, awkward actor in several school productions, but in college he developed real acting talent. His drama coach later said, "I wouldn't have been surprised if, after college, he had gone on to New York or Hollywood looking for a job as an actor."

He was never an athletic star, but Nixon (shown here in the center of the top row) was an eager and energetic football player at Whittier College. (Whittier College.)

Student Leader

Like his acting ability, Richard's social life improved in college. When Nixon arrived at Whittier as a freshman, there was only one social club for male students on campus. It was called the Franklins, and its members were sons of wealthy or socially prominent families; they were said to wear tuxedos at club functions. At the urging of some of his fellow working-class students, Nixon promptly organized a social club of his own. It was, he said, for men who "had to work their way through college." The new club was called the Orthogonians. The group held spaghetti-and-beans feasts every month and sponsored parties.

Nixon was elected vice-president of the student body in his sophomore year and president in his senior year. One classmate recalled of Nixon's elections, "He wanted to win all the time; no matter what he was doing, he wanted to be a winner."

The election to student body president was a good example of Nixon's ability to win votes. He made a campaign promise that was very appealing but seemed impossible to fulfill: he promised to obtain permission from college officials to hold a dance every month, even though dancing was not allowed on campus because of the school's Quaker heritage. Nixon's excellent campaign speeches, polished by years of debate practice, won him the election. He then managed to persuade the school trustees that it would be better to let the students dance on campus then to have them sneak off to the "evil" dance halls of Los Angeles. The result was that a dance was held every month during Nixon's senior year.

Richard escorted Ola Florence Welsh, who was also a student at Whittier, to many of these social affairs. In fact, the two dated throughout their college years, although each of them also dated other people. But the differences in their personalities — Richard was serious and stiff, Ola was bubbly and outgoing — caused the relationship to become weaker rather than stronger. By the time they graduated from college, they were no longer dating. Many biographers have also noted that, although Richard had many acquaintances on campus, he did not form any close and lasting friendships. Many people felt that he was too busy, too shy, or too wrapped up in his own thoughts and concerns to open up to others.

An Early Prophecy

In spite of all of his extracurricular activities, Nixon never forgot that classes were the most important part of college. He remained an A student. His major was history, and one of his history professors had a profound influence on his career. This was Dr. Paul Smith, whom Nixon called "the greatest intellectual inspiration of my early years." Smith was a Republican who urged his students to think about the importance of leadership in government. He encouraged them to consider entering public office, and he certainly helped turn Nixon's thoughts in that direction.

In 1934 Richard Nixon graduated from Whittier College after four years on the honor roll. His college career had demonstrated his ambition, his desire to excel, his intelligence, and his determination. Now he wanted to take those qualities to a larger world than Whittier. He applied for a scholarship to a new law school, at Duke University in Durham, North Carolina, and asked several of his professors to write to Duke, recommending him for a scholarship. Among the letters was one from Walter Dexter, the president of Whittier College, that summed up the impression Nixon had made on all who knew him during his college years. It said, "I cannot recommend him too highly because I believe that Nixon will become one of America's important, if not great leaders." Dexter's words came true. Nixon did become one of the country's most important leaders of the century. First, though, he faced many more years of education and preparation. The next step took him to North Carolina.

Chapter 3
Law, Love, and War

Nixon's first year at Duke Law School was also the first real challenge to his confidence. He had been a star student in high school, and at Whittier College he had only to repeat the same performance in the same town with most of the same fellow students. But at Duke, Richard found himself away from his family for the first time, and he also found himself competing with bright, ambitious students like himself from all around the country.

Nixon's load of seven classes kept him in the library until late each night; he also worked in the library for 35 cents an hour to earn money for food, books, and clothing (his scholarship paid only for his classes). Several times during that first year, he admitted in letters to his family and to Ola Florence Welsh that he was afraid he was not going to make it at Duke.

A HARDWORKING LAW STUDENT

Despite his doubts and his financial anxiety, Nixon kept doing what he was best at — working without a break to achieve his goal. His long hours of study prompted one classmate to call him "the hardest-working man I ever met." And because he always looked serious and often wore a worried frown, classmates gave him the nickname "Gloomy Gus," after a comic-strip character of the time. His only relaxation came at Duke football games, where he cheered himself hoarse, and at daily handball games, which gave him the opportunity to take showers in the gym (to save money, he rented a room in a house that did not have indoor plumbing). Students and teachers who knew Nixon at this time remember him as being very private, very dedicated to success, and very solemn. These traits have been part of Nixon's character ever since.

Nixon's long hours of studying paid off. He finished his first year with good grades, and his scholarship was renewed. He went home to Whittier and worked in the family store for the summer, then returned to Duke for his second year with greater confidence. During that year, he was elected president of the school's student law association, and he wrote articles for the campus law magazine, called *Law and Contemporary Problems.*

Nixon's campaign for the law association presidency, his work for the magazine, and the hours he still spent working in the library to earn some money started to cut into his study time, however, and near the end of the school year he began to worry about his grades. This anxiety led to an incident where two fellow students boosted Nixon through a small window into the dean's office, where he unlocked a desk drawer and found the students' records. Nixon and his partners did not remove or change any of the records, but they did examine them, and Nixon discovered that, although he was not among the top three students in his year's class, he did have a B-plus average.

Richard spent the summer of 1936 again working at the family store in Whittier. For his third and final year at Duke, he shared a run-down farmhouse with three other law students. They called their ramshackle home Whippoorwill Manor. Nixon also joined a fraternity, was president of the student law association for the second year in a row, and was made a member of the Order of the Coif, which was a national association of honor students in law.

MAPPING THE FUTURE

When the 1936 Christmas vacation arrived, Nixon and several of his classmates scraped together enough money for a short trip to New York City—not to see the sights, but to look for jobs in the city's respected law firms. Only one firm showed any interest in Nixon, however, and Nixon himself was more interested in going to work for the Federal Bureau of Investigation. The dean of Duke Law School wrote a letter to J. Edgar Hoover, director of the FBI, praising Nixon's intelligence and character in generous terms. But when no job offer came from the FBI, the dean called Nixon into his office for a talk.

Dean Horack was one of the few people at Duke to whom Nixon had confided his interest in government and his growing dream of entering politics. Now Horack gave Nixon some advice. Forget looking for a glamorous law job in New York or Washington, he told the depressed young man. Go back to your hometown, get into a law firm, and work your way into politics there, where you are known and respected. Nixon decided to follow Horack's advice.

In the spring of 1937, Nixon graduated from Duke. He was the third-ranked student in a class of 25. His mother, father, brother Edward, and grandmother Milhous drove across the country to attend the graduation ceremony. Nixon showed them around the campus where he had spent three grueling years, then rode back to Whittier with them. He was determined to take and pass the California bar examination — the test that all lawyers wishing to practice in the state must pass.

California Lawyer

Nixon returned to California to find that his student days were not yet over. Candidates for the state bar exam attended a special class to prepare them for the test. It was taught at the University of Southern California campus, and when Nixon arrived at home, he learned that the class had already been in session for three months. He would have to study harder than he had ever done at Duke in order to catch up. Once again, Nixon proved that he was equal to the challenge, and once again he succeeded. In November 1937 he was sworn in as a practicing attorney in the state of California. Now all that remained was to get a job.

With the help of an old friendship between the Milhous and Bewley families, he began handling accident and divorce cases for the law firm of Wingert and Bewley. Nixon soon gained the confidence of the firm's partners and their clients and in 1939 was made a junior partner in the firm.

A Business Failure

About this time Nixon suffered a business setback, much like the one his father had experienced with his unfruitful lemon grove years before. Nixon persuaded a group of Whittier businessmen to invest in a company to produce frozen orange juice and ship it to the East Coast. Nixon was the president of the company, which was called Citra-Frost. Unfortunately, he was never of a mechanical or technical turn of mind, and he did not really understand the equipment and chemistry needed to freeze the juice properly. Bewley recalled that Nixon worked "like a dog" to make the company succeed, cutting and squeezing oranges all night after working in the law office all day. But the business failed, and Nixon lost not only all of his own savings but also the investments of his backers.

It was back to law full-time for Nixon, but the hardworking young attorney had not forgotten his dream of entering politics. He knew that in order to win a local election he had to make himself known to voters and win their admiration. He did this by joining clubs and organizations and by making dozens of speeches. He was a member of the 20–30 Club (a group of young businessmen) and president of three groups: the Orange County Association of Cities, the Whittier College Alumni Association, and the Duke University Alumni of California. He spoke to Lions and Kiwanis clubs all over the Los Angeles area, and he impressed most of his listeners with his intelligence, his serious manner, and his speaking skills. From modest beginnings such as these, Nixon knew, many politicians had risen to state and even national offices.

The demands of work and public speaking left Nixon with little free time, but he spent some of that time acting. In late 1937 he joined a small theater group in Whittier, but admitted to one acquaintance that he was less interested in having fun than in meeting people who might prove to be legal clients or useful political contacts. After a few months with the group, however, Nixon's interests changed.

"Love at First Sight"

In January 1938 the theater group to which Nixon belonged was preparing to present a play called *The Dark Tower.* Nixon was cast to play the role of the male lead. His co-star was a young schoolteacher who had just moved to Whittier and was making her first appearance with the drama group. Her name was Thelma Catherine Ryan, and Nixon asked her for a date on the night they met. "For me," he wrote later, "it was a case of love at first sight."

Thelma Catherine Ryan was a year older than Nixon; she was born on March 16, 1912, in Ely, Nevada. Since childhood she had been called "Pat," because her father was Irish and she celebrated her birthday on St. Patrick's Day, March 17. The Ryan family moved to California during Pat's childhood. Her mother died of cancer when Pat was 13; four years later, her father died of lung disease caused by years of working in copper mines.

After her father's death, Pat worked as a bank clerk to pay for a year of college, but then she decided to try her luck on the East Coast. In New York City she worked as a secretary and then as an X-ray technician. She managed to save some money and in 1933 returned to California, where she attended the University of Southern California.

Pat held a number of part-time jobs to help pay her college expenses. Like many attractive young women in California, she flirted with a career in movies. But although she managed to land tiny parts in *Becky Sharp* (1935) and *The Great Ziegfeld* (1936), it seemed clear that she was not going to become a Hollywood star. So, upon graduating with honors from USC, she took a teaching job in Whittier. She joined the Whittier Community Players and there met the young Richard Nixon.

A Persistent Wooer

Nixon continued to ask Pat for a date after every rehearsal, although she laughingly turned him down, saying she was "too busy" to go out with him. But Nixon was determined and persistent in his courtship, as in everything he did. He introduced himself to Pat's friends and made himself part of their social group. Although he was not a good skater, he forced himself to go ice-skating to please her.

From the start, Nixon wanted to marry Pat. He told her so the third time they rehearsed together, but she did not take him seriously. "I thought he was nuts or something," she later said. "I couldn't imagine anyone ever saying anything like that so suddenly." But Nixon's devoted attentions finally won her over, and she began dating him.

Nixon's mother and other relatives were not warmly enthusiastic about this independent young woman who had no family and was not a Quaker, but Nixon kept proposing to Pat. After dating for two years, she accepted him, although he had so little money that she had to help pay for her own wedding ring. "I knew he was going to get places," she said. "He had drive."

Pat agreed to be married in a Quaker ceremony, which pleased Hannah Nixon. The wedding took place on June 21, 1940, in Riverside, California. After the afternoon ceremony, the newlyweds took off by car for a two-week honeymoon in Mexico. Because they had only $200 to spend, they filled the trunk of their car with canned food—only to discover later that Pat's friends had removed all the labels from the cans. Every meal they ate during the honeymoon was a surprise, from pork and beans for breakfast to grapefruit slices for supper. Nixon later boasted that they had seen every cathedral in Mexico for "only $178."

WARTIME MOVES

Events around the nation and the world touched Nixon's life in the year after his marriage. World War II was raging in Europe, and the United States joined the war late in 1941. A few weeks later, at the beginning of 1942, Nixon and Pat moved to Washington, D.C.

Nixon moved to Washington to do his part in the American war effort. One of his former professors from Duke was an official of a federal agency called the Office of Price Administration (OPA). He offered Nixon a position in the agency for more than he was earning as a lawyer in Whittier. In addition, Nixon knew that he had to do *something* in the war if he was to have a future in politics; no one would later vote for a candidate who could be accused of shirking his duty to his country.

As someone who had been born and raised a Quaker, Nixon was entitled to avoid military service if he chose to do so—and Hannah Nixon's strong Quaker belief made her urge him not to enlist. For a while, the OPA seemed like a good way to contribute to the war effort without violating his mother's religious feelings.

Nixon later said that his experience in the OPA led him to believe that most government agencies were overstaffed and inefficient. In truth, however, he held his job there for only six months. In June 1942, after long discussions with Pat, he enlisted in the U.S. Navy, which was looking for lawyers to receive officers' commissions. He received his basic training in Rhode Island, where he met the man who was later to serve as his secretary of state, William P. Rogers. Then he was sent to a Naval Reserve station about as far from the water as it was possible to get: in Ottumwa, Iowa. After seven months in Ottumwa as assistant to the executive officer, Nixon received orders to ship out to the Pacific. Pat rented an apartment in San Francisco and got a job in the OPA office there.

Duty in the Pacific

Nixon spent the first few months of his war duty in the South Pacific Combat Air Transport Command (SCAT) in New Caledonia, a large tropical island not far from Australia. He was responsible for routine tasks such as filling out paperwork, but he enlivened his stay on the island by learning to play poker. Although he knew nothing about the game when he arrived there, he applied himself diligently to the serious study of poker and quickly became one of the best players on the base. By the end of the war, Nixon had accumulated at least $3,000 in winnings—possibly several times that much. He played honestly, but he became a master of bluffing and of knowing when to take risks.

In mid-1944 Nixon was transferred to Bougainville, a small base in the Solomon Islands. His unit then invaded Green Island, but no one was able to perform any wartime heroics because the Japanese had already retreated. Nixon later remarked that the only danger he faced was from giant stinging centipedes.

On Green Island, Nixon was a supply officer, responsible for getting supplies loaded onto planes. He established a reputation for being efficient and reliable, and he became popular with the men because he was occasionally able to scrounge some food that was not part of official military rations. He operated a stand called Nixon's Snack Shack, where he provided free hamburgers, ham dinners, and Australian beer to his own men and to weary flight crews who stopped at the island.

In the Pacific during World War II, Nixon held the naval rank of lieutenant commander, although he did not see combat. He later joked that the most vicious enemies he faced were giant centipedes. (Copyright *Washington Post;* reprinted by permission of the D.C. Public Library.)

The war gave Nixon experience in leading other men and the opportunity to amass some poker winnings. It also gave him the military background that he would need if he were to attempt a political career. But one thing the war did not give him was combat action and the opportunity to become a hero. Nevertheless, Nixon did what he was asked to do by the Navy with skill and integrity, and he displayed good leadership qualities. It was not his fault he had no chance to become a hero. Soon enough he would have a chance to prove himself in another arena, that of politics.

Chapter 4

Congressman on the Move

When World War II ended in 1945, thousands of American servicemen came home to pick up their lives where they had left off when they were called to fight overseas. Richard Nixon was one of them. He was eager to return to his law practice in Whittier, particularly after Pat became pregnant and he realized that he would soon have a family to support. But his driving ambition also made him look beyond Whittier and the law. He was convinced that he had a future in politics. And the opportunity to enter the world of politics came sooner than he expected. Even before he arrived in Whittier after his discharge from the Navy, he received an invitation from the Republican Party to enter his first political contest.

RUNNING FOR CONGRESS

A group of Whittier businessmen called the "Committee of 100" approached Nixon and asked him to run for the U.S. House of Representatives. If elected, he would represent the congressional district that included Whittier and parts of Los Angeles County. Many of the men on the committee had got-

ten to know Nixon through his legal practice, his member-
ships in civic organizations, or his many speeches. They were
impressed with his aggressive, hard-hitting style of speech-
making and with his sharp intelligence, and they decided that
he had a good chance to beat the Democratic candidate in
the congressional race.

That Democrat was Jerry Voorhis, who had served five
terms in the House of Representatives. Voorhis was very popular in California and had been a supporter of some social-
welfare programs that had been started under Democratic
President Franklin D. Roosevelt and were being continued
by his Democratic successor, President Harry S. Truman.
Nixon and other Republicans believed that many middle-class
Americans were growing tired of these programs and of the
high taxes that were needed to pay for them. These people
felt that now was the time for the Republican Party to begin
winning back control from the Democrats, who had been in
power in Washington for many years.

First Campaign

Before Nixon could throw himself wholeheartedly into his
first political battle, he had a private contest to win at home.
He knew that Pat was expecting them to spend their savings
on a new home so they could raise their family in Whittier
while he worked at his law practice. Now he wanted to take
at least part of that hard-earned savings fund and invest it
in a political campaign that would take him away from his
home and his law office for a great deal of time. And if he
won the campaign, he would have to live in Washington, D.C.
Furthermore, this campaign would be just the beginning of
what Nixon hoped would be a long career in politics.

Politics did not appeal to Pat. She said on more than
one occasion that the life of a politician's wife "would not

have been one that I would have chosen." But she also admitted that when Nixon told her about the opportunity, "I told him it was his decision and I would do what he liked." Pat did ask Nixon to agree to two conditions: that she would never have to make a political speech, and that their home would remain a quiet and private place for the family, not the scene of political meetings or publicity stunts. Nixon agreed. Then, at the end of 1945, Nixon's nomination by the Republican Party was confirmed. His first campaign got under way.

Although he was a beginner at political campaigning, Nixon had plenty of experience in proving himself under pressure, in winning debates, and in making personal sacrifices to achieve a goal. The campaign required him to do all of these things.

For one thing, Nixon found that although he had the verbal support of the Committee of 100 and the Republican Party, he received very little money from them to help pay for his campaign. He drew on his rapidly vanishing savings to pay the rent on a small office. Because he could not afford an office staff, Pat worked for him full-time, typing his campaign letters and brochures and distributing them by hand. Pat also had to make numerous appearances with Nixon at "coffee hours" for women's clubs and other organizations, where she gave most people the impression of being very shy and uncomfortable. She probably *was* uncomfortable, for her pregnancy was very advanced at the time. In fact, Nixon's first child, a daughter who was named Patricia and called Tricia, was born on February 21, 1946, about two months into the campaign.

Building a Political Image

In this first political battle, Nixon needed a strong image to build up his identity with the voters. Because Americans were proud of their victory in World War II, he emphasized his military service. This was especially effective because Voorhis had spent the war in the House of Representatives, so many of the young men who were coming home from war to vote for the first time felt that Nixon was "one of them."

But the military image was not enough to support the whole campaign. Nixon needed something else, something that would carry him not just to victory against Voorhis but also to other political triumphs later. He sized up the mood of the country and decided that anticommunism would win votes. By taking a strong anti-Communist position, Nixon established an identity that would carry him through many campaigns on an amazingly swift rise to power. In order to understand Nixon's anti-Communist campaign against Voorhis, it is important to know something about the changing feelings of Americans toward the Soviet Union and its Communist government and way of life.

THE FEAR OF COMMUNISM

Communism, at its most basic, is a system of government and economics in which land, factories, and other sources of productivity are owned not by individuals but by the central government, which then controls the flow of money and goods. In theory, the goal of communism is equal distribution of wealth so that there are no rich citizens and no poor ones – although no Communist nation has succeeded in making the theories of communism work smoothly in real life. The typical effect of communism has been to create large, powerful central governments, sometimes called totalitarian governments, that control many aspects of individual citizens' lives and sometimes deny them basic human rights.

From the time communism gained control in the Soviet Union in the early 1900s, a majority of Americans felt that the Communist way of life was alien and opposed to the American way of life. Communism banned private property, but capitalism, the economic basis of American and European cultures, was based on private property and ambition. Furthermore, Americans valued individuality and the freedoms guaranteed to them in the Bill of Rights – freedoms that most Americans felt were painfully lacking in the Soviet Union.

However, starting in October 1929 and extending throughout the 1930s, a severe economic depression gripped the United States. Banks closed, thousands of people lost their savings, businesses collapsed, jobs were wiped out, and the country experienced widespread suffering. Many people blamed this economic disaster on rich capitalists, such as bankers, factory-owners, and stock-market investors.

At this time, some Americans found the Communist theory of equal distribution of wealth to be an attractive alternative to capitalism. Many writers, artists, labor-union workers, and university professors spoke out against capitalism as the cause of unfairness and poverty, and a number of these people flirted with communism or even joined the American Communist Party. Because the Soviet Communists had adopted the color red as their symbol, these people were called "reds" if they were out-and-out Communists and "pinkos" if they sympathized with Communist ideas or were influenced by them.

Wartime Allies, Peacetime Enemies

The Soviet Union and the United States were allies in World War II, fighting side by side against their common enemy, Nazi Germany. But by that time, many of the Americans who had once been impressed by Communist theories had changed their minds about the Soviet Union because of the cruelty, prejudice, and repression that flourished there, especially under Soviet leader Josef Stalin. In addition, there were fears that the Soviet Union would take over other nations after the war in order to set itself up as a rival to the United States in world politics—which is exactly what did happen.

As soon as World War II ended, the United States and its former ally, the Soviet Union, entered a period of mutual rivalry, suspicion, and enmity that is usually called the "Cold War." It was an era of bomb shelters in family basements and of fears that the advance of communism would eventually reach America's own shores. It also was an era of strong, renewed anti-Communist feelings in the United States. "Red-baiting," or attacking the Communists and anyone who sympathized with them, became part of political life.

Nixon's hatred of communism was genuine, but he also was shrewd enough to see that red-baiting would get him a lot of attention and would make him popular with the growing number of Americans who feared the Soviets. From a Navy lieutenant in the "stinking jungles" of the Pacific, he turned himself into a relentless soldier in the Cold War, ready to attack communism and anything that resembled it. But being opposed to communism in general was not quite enough. He had to go one step further and turn anticommunism into a personal attack on his opponents. He was sure that he could defeat any candidate who he believed was a red or a pinko. This would be the basis of his attack on Voorhis.

Campaign Strategy

Nixon got off to a dramatic start. In the first of five debates with Voorhis, he accused Voorhis of being controlled by Communist sympathizers in one of the nation's largest labor unions, the Congress of Industrial Organizations (CIO). When Voorhis indignantly denied the charge, Nixon dramatically pulled from his pocket a newspaper clipping that said that a local branch of the CIO had spoken out in favor of Voorhis. Although Voorhis protested that he had not asked the CIO for its support and could not prevent the union from expressing its opinion, Nixon had succeeded in making Voorhis look shifty and dishonest. This set the pattern for the rest of the campaign. Refusing to debate any of the other issues that faced California voters, Nixon hammered away at what he believed to be Voorhis' Communist sympathies, telling voters that Voorhis cast his votes in Congress the way labor leaders and other probable Communists told him to.

Nixon's attack on Voorhis consisted of two parts. First, he claimed that Voorhis was controlled by the CIO; second, he claimed that the CIO was influenced or controlled by Communists. Although he did not offer a shred of real evidence to support either of these claims, Nixon played up to the fears of many middle-class professionals and businessmen that social-welfare programs and labor unions were communistic in nature. True, Communist influence *did* exist in some labor unions and in some social programs, but Nixon exaggerated the amount and importance of that influence.

The campaign was marred by some very dirty political tactics. One of the most unpleasant events during the campaign occurred when hundreds of voters in the district received anonymous phone calls from callers who said, "Did you know Jerry Voorhis is a Communist?" and then hung up. Nixon denied any knowledge of such calls and said that if his supporters made them, it was without his approval.

Whether his campaign was dishonest, as his enemies say, or merely aggressive, as his supporters say, Nixon won his first election. He received 56 percent of the vote to become Whittier's new representative when Congress met again in 1947. When his term ended two years later, no one ran against him, and he was re-elected for a second two-year term.

CONGRESSIONAL CAREER

Most junior congressmen do not expect to do much during their first terms in Congress. Nixon, however, was more active than most. The Republicans were in control of the House of Representatives for the first time since the early 1930s, and Nixon's friends on the Committee of 100 wrote letters to important Republicans in the House asking them to help Nixon along. But the new congressman did not rely on help from others. He went after every chance there was to make himself busy and important.

Nixon was the only first-term congressman to be appointed to a special congressional committee that went to Europe to study the damage done by World War II to the economies of several countries. He later voted in favor of U.S. aid to rebuild the economies of Turkey and Greece. He also served on the House of Representatives' Labor and Education Committee, where he helped write a bill called the Taft-Hartley Act of 1947, which spelled out new rules for relations between labor unions and company owners (the act strengthened the power of the company owners). Without a doubt, however, the activity that was most important to Nixon during his time in the House was his membership in the House Committee on Un-American Activities (usually called HUAC). Nixon's connection with HUAC was to boost him almost overnight into national fame.

HUAC and Hiss

Nixon managed to be appointed to HUAC, although positions on the committee were in great demand. Even in his first year in the House, he had a reputation as one who looked for Communists everywhere and attacked anyone who could be suspected of Communist ties.

Before and following World War II, HUAC had been holding hearings to investigate people who were accused of being Communists. Critics of the hearings called them "witch hunts" because at times they seemed similar to the hysterical, prejudiced Salem witch trials of colonial days. Citizens who were summoned to testify before the HUAC hearings often were pressured to name friends or acquaintances who might be Communists. If they refused to give names, they could be fined or sent to jail, even though they protested that individual political beliefs were not against the law and were protected by the Bill of Rights. The hearings received a great deal of excited attention, but they did not produce much in the way of results. Then, in 1948, a shocking spy case investigated by HUAC made Richard Nixon a national figure in the war on communism.

In the course of a summer hearing, HUAC members were electrified by testimony from a man named Whittaker Chambers, who was once a senior editor for *Time* magazine. Chambers confessed that during the 1930s he had been a member of the American Communist Party. When the committee asked him to name other American Communists, he made an astonishing disclosure. He said that Alger Hiss had been a Communist, too.

Alger Hiss, one of the 20th century's most controversial figures, was a friend of many of America's powerful, educated, and wealthy men. He was a graduate of Harvard Law School, and he had served as secretary to Oliver Wendell Holmes, perhaps the most famous Supreme Court justice of all. Hiss also had been a member of the U.S. State Department. He was an advisor to the United Nations and the president of a well-respected organization called the Carnegie Endowment for International Peace.

In short, with his cultivated background and his position of privilege and prominence, Hiss was the last person who might have been suspected of being a communist. Chambers caused a further sensation when he announced that Hiss had secretly passed U.S. government documents to agents of

Holding the HUAC committee spellbound with his shocking revelations, Whittaker Chambers announces that the popular Alger Hiss is a Communist spy. (Copyright *Washington Post;* reprinted by permission of the D.C. Library.)

the Soviet Union. Alger Hiss a spy? The nation waited breathlessly to see him grilled in front of HUAC.

Hiss appeared before the committee and denied Chambers' accusation. His confident, polished manner won over most of the committee members. These members began to think that Chambers, not Hiss, was lying. Perhaps they had gone too far in accusing such a prominent person of espionage. Nixon, however, was not impressed. He sensed that there were weaknesses in Hiss' case.

The Pumpkin Papers

Nixon decided to go after Hiss, even though some of his political advisors warned him that a mistake in judgment could cost him his political future. He got himself appointed chairman of a special committee to investigate the Hiss case. During the next half year, he spent hundreds of hours with Chambers, listening to the former Communist's tales of activities years earlier, trying to find a way to prove Hiss' guilt. During this time, he became firmly convinced that Hiss was a traitor. "If the American people understood the real character of Alger Hiss," he once said, "they would boil him in oil."

The problem with the Hiss case was that Chambers himself was not a very reliable witness. Many observers believed that he was lying about Hiss in order to turn attention away from his own past misdeeds, including communism and espionage. Finally, just when President Truman was urging HUAC to dismiss the case for lack of evidence and Nixon was putting pressure on Chambers to produce proof of his accusations, the long-awaited proof appeared. Chambers produced microfilmed copies of secret State Department documents that he claimed he had received from Hiss to pass on to his Soviet contacts. The most incriminating set of papers came to be called the "pumpkin papers" because Chambers said that Hiss hid them inside a hollowed-out pumpkin on Chambers' farm.

Senator McCarthy's Blacklists

About the time of Nixon's success in the Hiss case, when the country was filled with fears of Communist spies, a fiery Wisconsin senator named Joseph McCarthy gained great influence over the House Committee on Un-American Activities. Although McCarthy's period of real power lasted only from about 1950 to 1954, he gave the name of "McCarthyism" to a decade or more of American history. The "McCarthy era" included the late 1940s and the early 1950s. These were the years during the Cold War between the United States and the Soviet Union when McCarthy and his colleagues on HUAC fought against communism in America's movies, colleges, armed forces, and elsewhere.

Another name for McCarthyism is the "red scare." McCarthy and those who shared his views convinced many people that Communists were all around, working to undermine the American way of life. Unfortunately, in trying to identify and root out American communism, they often violated the civil rights of American citizens, and they created a poisonous atmosphere of fear and hatred that lingered for many years.

Some actual charges of espionage were made during the McCarthy era. The best-known case was that of Julius and Ethel Rosenberg, who were executed for treason in 1953. For the most part, however, the McCarthyites concentrated on interrogating and harassing people whose only "crime" was that at one time they had joined the Communist Party, or had known someone who at one time had belonged to the Communist Party, or were accused by someone else of having been members of the Communist Party. In this swirling fog of suspicion and vague accusations, some people suffered unjustly. For example, the movie industry was believed to be filled with Communist writers and directors, so a group of these people called the "Hollywood Ten" was sent to jail for refusing to answer HUAC's questions about communism in Hollywood.

But perhaps the most vicious and hurtful aspect of McCarthyism was the so-called "blacklists." To blacklist someone means to place his or her name on a list of people who will be denied certain rights or privileges. McCarthy and his supporters drew up blacklists containing hundreds of names and claimed that they were all Communists. In many cases, the blacklisted person's connection with communism was extremely remote or even completely untrue. Yet the lists were widely circulated, and because of the fear with which people regarded the powerful HUAC, they had a widespread effect. Many people—writers, actors, college professors, teachers, and others—lost their jobs with no chance to defend themselves because their names appeared on a blacklist. Books were banned from public libraries, people became afraid to speak up in favor of the traditional American right to free speech, and some careers were ruined forever by Joe McCarthy's blacklists.

McCarthy's fall from power came in 1954, when he attempted to prove that the Army was infected with communism among its officers. For the first time, HUAC hearings were shown on television, and the American people saw McCarthy's behavior as brutal, insulting, illogical, and dictatorial. The red scare continued; in fact, that same year Congress passed a law that banned the American Communist Party. But McCarthy's hold on the nation's fearful imagination was broken, and the hysteria he had created began slowly to fade. He died in 1957, still claiming that the U.S. government was filled with Communist spies.

A Questionable Verdict

This evidence greatly strengthened Nixon's case against Hiss. Eventually, a federal court charged Hiss with perjury for having lied to HUAC (he could not be charged with espionage because the spying incidents had taken place too many years previously to be covered by the law). Confronted with the evidence that Nixon had obtained from Chambers, Hiss lost much of his coolness and made an unfavorable appearance in court, stammering in confusion and contradicting himself repeatedly. Although the first jury in his trial was unable to decide on a verdict, a second jury was called. In January of 1950 this jury found Hiss guilty of perjury.

Hiss went to prison for 44 months. After being released on parole, he became a salesman in New York City. He continued to protest that he was innocent and that he had been framed by Chambers, and many people believed him. In 1975, the Massachusetts Bar Association restored his license to practice law in that state.

To this day, the question of Hiss' innocence or guilt cannot be answered with certainty. Historians still debate the case. But one thing that cannot be questioned is the effect that the Hiss case had on Richard Nixon's political career. "The Hiss case," Nixon himself has said, "for the first time, forcibly demonstrated to the American people that domestic Communism was a real and present danger to the security of the nation." Strengthened by his victory over Hiss, Nixon would use the public's fear of communism in the United States again in 1950 to help him in his next big step toward the White House.

Chapter 5

Into the National Spotlight

The year 1948 was an important one for Nixon in several ways. For one thing, it was the year of a family event. The Nixons became parents for the second time when daughter Julie was born in Washington in July. But the busy father had little time to spend with his two young daughters, for his congressional duties and his HUAC activities kept him working late into the night and on most weekends. Fortunately, he did not have to take time to campaign for re-election to his seat in the House of Representatives. He had become so popular in his home district that he won the 1948 congressional race easily.

During the entire second half of the year, the Hiss investigation occupied almost all of Nixon's attention and time. To please Pat, he did agree to go on a short vacation cruise to Panama in December, but he left the cruise ship by helicopter on the second night after he received a telegram announcing that Chambers had produced the dramatic "pumpkin papers." Nixon was urgently needed in Washington to help prepare the government's case against Hiss for trial. Sitting at the captain's table aboard the cruise ship, Pat gallantly threw her hands into the air and said with a smile, "Here we go again." Throughout Nixon's career, this patient, uncomplaining attitude on Pat's part made it possible for him to give all his energy to politics.

THE 1950 SENATE RACE

The Hiss affair introduced Nixon to the thrill of being the center of national attention. When the excitement of the investigation and the hearings began to die down, being a junior congressman in the House of Representatives seemed dull by comparison. Nixon wanted to move into the Senate, which traditionally is regarded as more important and powerful than the House—and he wanted to do it quickly, while the glamour of the Hiss case was still clinging to his name. Although some of his friends in the Committee of 100 and in Washington advised him not to make any hasty moves that could backfire in failure, Nixon was determined to make his own decisions. He announced that he would run for one of California's two Senate seats in 1950.

The Republican Party agreed to nominate Nixon *if* he could convince the state's Republican leaders that he was popular enough to win the Senate race. Much depended upon the outcome of Hiss' trial. If the jury found Hiss innocent, Nixon would be forever associated with a mistake in judgment and a failure. But the jury found Hiss guilty, and one of Nixon's supporters crowed gleefully, "Nixon could whip Abraham Lincoln, if necessary, in the senator fight!" Nixon received the nomination.

A Campaign of Allegations

Nixon's opponent was not Abraham Lincoln, of course. She was a Democrat named Helen Gahagan Douglas, who had once been an opera singer and who was married to a popular movie actor named Melvyn Douglas. Like Nixon, she had served in the House of Representatives and wanted to move on to the Senate. Nixon set out to defeat her the same way he had defeated Voorhis. The result was a campaign that is said by many historians to be one of the dirtiest and most dishonest in the history of modern politics.

In 1950, the red scare was at its height. The Hiss case and other HUAC investigations had frightened many Americans into believing that there was a Communist conspiracy to steal control of the government. Nixon knew that if he could make people think that Douglas was tainted with communism, he would win the election. After all, it had worked with Voorhis.

Nixon toured California in a station wagon, with Pat riding in the back seat and an aide driving. He made countless speeches and sent copies of them to the newspapers. In every speech, he drove home the need to stamp out the Communist influence in American government.

As the campaign progressed, Nixon told audiences that Douglas had "a soft attitude toward communism," saying that she had "voted the Communist Party line in Congress." He played on the widespread fear that the movie industry was a hotbed of communism by reminding audiences that Douglas was married to an actor, and he joked about celebrities getting into politics. One of Douglas' supporters was an actor named Ronald Reagan, who was interested in politics and was a Democrat. Later he would become a Republican and 40th President of the United States.

The "Pink Sheet" and the "Pink Lady"

As with Voorhis, Nixon's allegations (charges) against Douglas were vague and hard to prove or disprove. It was a matter of record that she opposed HUAC and its activities, for example, and in Nixon's eyes that meant she must support communism. Many Americans, including President Truman himself, disapproved of HUAC and the way it operated, but this did not make them Communists or "pinkos." But time and again Nixon hammered home the image of Douglas as a Communist sympathizer, without ever offering proof. He printed up 500,000 copies of a document on pink paper and spread them around the state. The "Pink Sheet," as it was called, claimed to show that Douglas was a Communist by giving details of her congressional voting record. Like Nixon's speeches, however, it was a collection of vague hints without any clear proof.

Some of Nixon's tactics were extremely crude. He called Douglas the "Pink Lady," a name that not only reminded his listeners of Douglas' supposed pro-Communist attitude but also reminded them that she was a woman—and in 1950 many Americans felt that a woman's place was *not* in the Senate. Some Democrats joined Nixon's supporters, even though he was a Republican, because they did not like the idea of a woman in the Senate. One of these was Jack Kennedy, a young Democratic politician from Boston who would one day be Nixon's biggest rival. Kennedy gave Nixon $1,000 as a campaign contribution to help him beat Douglas.

"Tricky Dick"

As the campaign went on, it seemed that Nixon enjoyed belittling the fact that Douglas was a woman. He ended many of his attacks on her by saying that she was "pink right down to her underwear." But he displayed the talent he had shown as a college debater by wriggling away from direct questions that might challenge his claims about Douglas' link with the Communists.

Nixon's questionable methods won him a nickname during the campaign. It is not clear who first called him "Tricky Dick"; some people say that it was Helen Douglas herself. Whatever the source, the nickname soon appeared in the *Independent Review,* a small southern newspaper. It stayed with Nixon for the rest of his career.

Happy Days

Historians and political writers have accused both Nixon and Douglas of dirty fighting in the 1950 senatorial campaign. Douglas' own tactics were not spotlessly clean. She made foolish errors in attacking Nixon's voting record in Congress, which made her look careless and ill-informed, and she recklessly compared Nixon to Hitler and Stalin, which made her look shrill and excitable. Although she tried to run a tough campaign, she was no match for Nixon's smooth style of verbal combat, polished over years of debate practice.

On election day, Nixon beat Douglas by 680,000 votes. His victory margin was the largest of anyone elected to the Senate that year. Pat later remembered Nixon's joyous excitement on election night: "We hopped from party to party far into the night," she said. "Dick was so exuberant. Wherever there was a piano, he played 'Happy Days Are Here Again.' "

A few weeks later, Nixon received a lucky break. The California senator whose seat he and Douglas had been competing for decided to retire early, so Nixon was able to enter the Senate several months ahead of all the other junior senators who had been elected in 1950. When he took his Senate seat in January of 1951, he was 38 years old — the youngest of the nation's new senators.

SENATOR NIXON

The Hiss case and the aggressive campaign against Douglas made Nixon one of the best-known of the young senators. His reputation was based on his strong stand against communism, and his fellow Republicans expected him to continue that stand in the Senate. They appointed him to the Permanent Investigations Subcommittee, which was the Senate's version of HUAC. Joseph McCarthy was the chairman of the subcommittee. But during 1951 and 1952, Nixon was busier outside the Senate than inside it.

Because of his victories over Voorhis and Douglas, his publicity in the Hiss case, and his excellent speech-making skills, Nixon became the most popular speaker in the Republican Party. Wherever he went, people flocked to hear him. And Nixon simply loved to campaign — if not for himself, then for any Republican who needed his help to win votes. He crisscrossed the country in a fever of activity, making speeches that attacked the Democrats and Communists and boosted the Republicans. In 1951, he made a speech almost every other day and appeared in at least 25 states. On Lincoln's birthday alone, he spoke in Philadelphia, Louisville, Grand Rapids, and St. Paul. The work of keeping Nixon's busy schedule straight fell to his new secretary, Rose Mary Woods, who had worked for several congressmen. Nixon invited her to join his staff when he became a senator. Rose Mary Woods was to be a loyal employee and a friend to both Nixon and Pat for many years to come.

All of Nixon's speaking appearances helped the Republican Party, but Nixon knew that one day they would help him directly. The candidates whom he helped get elected were grateful. So were the party organizers who raised money on his speeches. During his two years in the Senate, Nixon built up a solid base of loyalty among Republicans all over the country. This gave him support outside his home state — support that would be needed to make Nixon a national, rather than a state, political leader. And the leap into national importance was just around the corner.

THE PRESIDENTIAL CAMPAIGN OF 1952

During Nixon's term in the Senate, the Republicans were loud in their criticism of Democratic President Harry Truman, and Nixon was one of the loudest. He did not approve of the way Truman handled the Korean War, which began in 1950 when the Communist forces of North Korea attacked U.S.-supported South Korea. Nixon favored an all-out attack on the northern Communists, including bombing their strongholds across the border in China. But Truman handled the war in a more cautious manner, hoping to keep a local war from turning into another World War. Nixon, however, felt that Truman was making it easy for Communists to take over all of Asia. For this and other reasons, the Republicans were delighted when Truman announced that he would not run for re-election in 1952. They were determined to put their own man in the White House, and most people had a pretty good idea who that man would be.

Dwight D. Eisenhower, the general who had led the Allied forces in Europe to victory in World War II, was one of the best-loved war heroes in American history. After the war, he served as commander of the newly formed alliance called the North Atlantic Treaty Organization (NATO). His career had been entirely military; indeed, he had never held an elected office or served in civilian government. But the public had such a high opinion of him that most observers felt he could win a presidential election. By early 1952, many people expected that the Republican Party would name Eisenhower as its candidate. The question was: Who would be the candidate for Vice-President?

Ike and Dick

In May of 1952, Governor Thomas Dewey of New York attended a Republican dinner where he was impressed with a speech made by Nixon. Dewey was one of the managers of Eisenhower's campaign, and he suggested to Ike (as Eisenhower was called) that Nixon would make a good running mate. Nixon had experience in both the House of Representatives and the Senate (although this experience totaled only six years), he was a superb speaker and a loyal Republican who would be valuable during the presidential campaign, he was young (to balance Ike's maturity), and he was from California, the nation's second most populous state and therefore the home of many voters. Eisenhower agreed to Nixon as his vice-presidential candidate.

Pat was not happy at the thought of another political campaign. The long drives and crowded assemblies of the Douglas campaign were only two years in the past, and she had been looking forward to a more settled family life during Nixon's Senate term. She tried hard to talk Nixon out of accepting the offer to run for Vice-President. At the Republican National Convention, he spent one whole night arguing with her about it, even calling his campaign manager to come to their hotel room to reason with Pat at 4 A.M. in the morning. She finally said, "I guess I can make it through another campaign," but she hoped until the last minute that he would change his mind and decide not to run. The next day, she was at a restaurant with a friend when she heard a news bulletin announcing that General Eisenhower had just selected Nixon to be his running mate.

The Republican National Convention was a triumph for Eisenhower, who received his party's nomination in the face of some stiff competition from Senator Robert Taft of Ohio. And it was a triumph for Nixon, who, at the age of 39, had found a place in the 1952 presidential campaign alongside one of the most popular men in America. When it was announced on the convention floor who the vice-presidential candidate would be, television and news cameras zoomed in on Ike and Nixon (this was the first national political convention to be shown on television). Photographs taken at that moment show the two men holding their joined hands in the air. Just six years after entering politics, Nixon was a candidate for the second-highest office in the land. He could not know that a few weeks later he would face the possibility of being thrown out of the Republican campaign.

The Slush Fund

The crisis that almost kept Nixon from becoming Vice-President had to do with money. Political campaigning is expensive, and all candidates accept contributions to help pay for their campaign expenses. It is understood, however, that money contributed to a campaign is not supposed to be for the candidate's personal use. Furthermore, all contributions are supposed to be a matter of public record. In this way, citizens can see who gives money to politicians and how much is given. The idea is to prevent someone or some group from secretly giving money to a candidate in return for political favors after the candidate is elected. Money that is not correctly accounted for, or that may be used for the candidate's private expenses, is sometimes called a "slush fund." One of the most damaging accusations any politician can face is that he accepted or used money improperly or that he has a slush fund.

In the middle of the 1952 campaign, therefore, Nixon was shocked and deeply disturbed when he saw the September 18 issue of the *New York Post*. A huge headline read, "SECRET NIXON FUND!" A slightly smaller headline beneath that one read, "Secret Rich Men's Trust Fund Keeps Nixon in Style Far Beyond His Salary." The headlines referred to a fund of about $18,000 that consisted of cash contributions from Nixon's supporters, some of whom went all the way back to the Committee of 100 in Whittier. The suggestion was that wealthy and powerful Republicans had given Nixon money to use in whatever way he wanted—in short, that they had bought him.

Most politicians, however, have some sort of a cash pool to pay their campaign expenses. Nixon said that he had had this fund for several years and used the money to pay for such campaign expenses as hotel rooms, printing costs, and airplane tickets. He claimed that the money came in the form of small donations to his campaign staff, not large payments to himself. And the fund was not "secret," he protested; he simply had not told anyone about it because he thought no one would be interested.

A Campaign in Trouble

Nixon and Eisenhower had boasted that their campaign was "a crusade for political purity" and that they would drive "the Democratic crooks" out of Washington. Now they found themselves on the defensive, as the Democrats let fly with charges that Nixon was corrupt and lining his pockets with shady deals. The slush fund quickly overshadowed communism and every other issue and became the focus of the campaign. Some Democrats, including President Truman and Adlai Stevenson, the Democratic presidential candidate, said that Nixon should be formally investigated or even charged with illegal use of campaign funds.

Suddenly Eisenhower was under tremendous pressure from many Republicans to drop Nixon from his campaign. They wanted Ike to win, and they felt that the scandal over Nixon was hurting his chances. But Ike stood by his commitment and refused to dump Nixon. Nixon, Ike declared, should be given a chance to clear himself of the charges. But Ike added that Nixon would remain on the Republican ticket *only* if he could prove himself to be "cleaner than a hound's tooth." Now it was up to Nixon to fight back against the greatest threat to his career that he had yet faced.

The "Checkers" Speech

Nixon decided that the best way to fight back against the accusations being made against him was to take his case directly to the American people. He would use television, which was a brand-new force in politics, to make a speech (the Republican National Committee paid for the broadcast, which cost about $75,000). Nixon agreed with Republican leaders that if the public response to his speech was favorable, he would remain on the Republican ticket. If it was unfavorable, however, he would withdraw. With his political future hanging on the outcome of a half-hour broadcast, Nixon showed up at a TV studio four days after the *Post* article appeared. The speech made television and political history.

More than 58 million people watched the speech. They saw a nervous but intense Nixon lay his personal life bare. He began by admitting that the $18,000 fund did exist, but he explained that he used it only for "political expenses that I did not think should be charged to the taxpayers of the United States." He then gave a detailed account of everything he owned and all his mortgages and debts, in order to prove that he had not made himself rich on cash contributions. He even challenged the Democratic presidential and vice-presidential candidates to do the same.

Nixon also wanted to show that he and his family had a simple, average, all-American lifestyle—not a flashy, rich one—so he pointed out that Pat did not even have a mink coat. She had "a respectable Republican cloth coat," he said, and added with a grin, "But I always tell her that she'd look good in anything." To drive home the point, Nixon repeated a quote from Abraham Lincoln about how the Lord must have liked the common people because he made so many of them.

Nixon did make one humorous "confession." He admitted that he had accepted a personal gift from a supporter in Texas. Looking into the camera, he said, "You know what it was? It was a little cocker spaniel dog in a crate that he sent all the way from Texas. Black and white spotted. And our little girl—Tricia, the six-year-old—named it 'Checkers.' And, you know, the kids love that dog and I just want to say this right now, that whatever they say about it, we're going to keep him."

Nixon concluded the broadcast by telling the television audience that they should write or telegraph the Republican National Committee with their verdict on his candidacy. He then left the studio, convinced that the speech had been not just an extreme personal humiliation but also a political failure. "I loused it up," he said to his campaign managers, "and I'm sorry." But Nixon was quite wrong. Although a few critics argued that the "Checkers" speech was just another example of Nixon's ability to mislead the public, most viewers felt that he was sincere and honest. The dog-loving American public responded to his speech with more than 300,000 favorable letters and telephone calls. The next day, Ike greeted Nixon with a beaming smile and said, "You're my boy." Nixon's hold on the vice-presidential nomination was secure.

Chapter 6

The Vice-Presidency

Winning the vice-presidential nomination was one thing. Now it was time to win the election. Eisenhower did little campaigning. He was not strongly linked to the Republican Party. In fact, he hoped to be elected as an "American President" rather than as a "Republican President." So it was left to Nixon to prove his worth as a party campaigner, and he did so without hesitation.

A FIGHTING CAMPAIGNER

Nixon made dozens of speeches around the nation. The Democrats continued to ask him embarrassing questions about the slush fund, but after the success of the "Checkers" speech, Nixon was sure that the American public was behind him. He lashed back at his Democratic opponents with scorn, returning to his old theme of Communist sympathizers in the Democratic Party.

His insults and attacks on Democratic politicians earned Nixon many enemies. One was President Truman, who was enraged by a speech Nixon made in which he called Truman a "traitor" to American principles. Truman never forgave Nixon, and nearly a decade later he told a reporter that Nixon was "a shifty-eyed . . . liar."

Nixon's fiery, fighting style of campaigning was privately encouraged by Eisenhower, but in public Eisenhower often toned down some of Nixon's wilder statements. This had the effect of making Eisenhower appear even-tempered and fair-minded, while Nixon was hot-headed and argumentative. From the start, the differences in style and beliefs of the two men prevented them from forming a close partnership or friendship. Nixon, who felt that he was expected to do all the dirty work for Eisenhower and the Republicans, later thought that Eisenhower should have been more grateful to him.

But the personal distance that existed between the two candidates did not hurt their campaign. Ike's popularity was so great that the Democratic presidential candidate, Adlai Stevenson, did not have a chance. On election day, nearly six million Democrats crossed party lines to vote Republican. Eisenhower and Nixon won by an overwhelming majority. Nixon, only 39 years old, had become the second-youngest Vice-President in the nation's history (the youngest was James Buchanan's Vice-President, John Breckinridge, who took office at age 36 in 1857).

FIRST TERM

During Nixon's first term as Vice-President (1953–1957), his main responsibility was to keep peace among the various groups within the Republican Party. Because Eisenhower was not really a party politician, Nixon was the man to whom

During his first year as Vice-President, Nixon visited American soldiers stationed in Korea as part of the U.S war effort there. (Nixon Project, National Archives.)

party leaders looked to promote Republican interests in the White House. One of his most difficult tasks was trying to control Republican Senator Joe McCarthy.

McCarthy's increasingly wild accusations about Communist conspiracies inside the government had become an embarrassment to Eisenhower and to the Republicans. Nixon hated the idea of American communism as much as McCarthy did, but Nixon was a party politician first and last. He did not want Republicans to weaken the party by attacking other Republicans. He tried to tone down some of McCarthy's sweeping attacks on church leaders and on government workers in the Eisenhower administration. But when McCarthy attacked the U.S. Army, even Nixon knew that it was political suicide to be too closely associated with the senator from Wisconsin. McCarthy's power was broken when the Senate officially censured (criticized) him in 1954, and Nixon hoped that the public would forget his own links with McCarthy.

Nixon was not the first Vice-President to discover that being the nation's second-highest official is not as exciting as it sounds. He had hoped for an active role, helping to shape Eisenhower's policies and decisions, but he never became one of the inner circle of the President's Cabinet members and advisors. In truth, Eisenhower saw no need to involve Nixon in the day-to-day business of running the country. At first, Nixon's duties were largely limited to his ceremonial role of presiding over the Senate. He did not have an office at the White House, and he received less money to pay his staff than he had received as a senator for this purpose.

On the Road Again

Nixon had a chance to shine in 1954, when congressional elections were held. As he had done before, he lent his services to the campaigns of many Republicans who were running for the House of Representatives, the Senate, or state legislatures. And he proved that he was capable of an almost superhuman workload by traveling 26,000 miles in one 48-day period, during which he made 204 speeches and gave more than 100 interviews in 95 cities in 31 states.

During the 1954 campaign, Nixon's speeches were his old standbys: the good work of the Republicans, whom he said were fighting Communist influence in government, and the stupidity of the Democrats, whom he called tools of the "Communist conspiracy." However, Nixon's hard-hitting style did not work this time. McCarthy's growing unpopularity had made his style of smug red-baiting less popular, but Nixon refused to talk about anything else. The election returns were not good news for the Republicans. The Democrats won the majority of seats in both the House and the Senate. From then on, Eisenhower's Republican administration had to work with a Congress that was dominated by Democrats.

Party Battles

When Eisenhower announced his intention to run for re-election in 1956, Nixon took it for granted that he would be Ike's running mate for the second time. Thus, he was deeply shaken when the President's advisors made several attempts to dump him from the ticket. These advisors thought that Nixon was too argumentative and too fond of name-calling and mud-slinging. They wanted a statesman, someone with a more polished image who had not been tainted with inquiries into his finances, to run with the President. Once again, however, Ike would not ask Nixon to back down, although he hoped that Nixon would volunteer to do so.

Nixon, however, was not about to back down. He hung on grimly, calling upon all the Republican leaders whom he

President Eisenhower (left) had hoped that Nixon would drop out of the 1956 campaign. When Nixon did not do so, however, the President smilingly stood side-by-side with him at the Republican National Convention. (Library of Congress.)

had helped in previous campaigns to give him their support, and he won the vice-presidential nomination for the second time. But some oberservers noticed that Nixon's 1956 campaign speeches were calmer and more subdued than those in the past.

Although Nixon had called Adlai Stevenson a Communist in 1952, he did not do so when Stevenson again ran as the Democratic candidate for President in 1956. Some reporters called him "the New Nixon"; others claimed that the change in his style was only skin-deep, not sincere. It seemed clear, however, that Nixon saw a need to polish up his own image in order to survive in politics. As in 1952, the Eisenhower-Nixon ticket won an easy victory over the Democrats in 1956.

SECOND TERM

During his second term as Vice-President (1957–1961), Nixon faced what is perhaps the most difficult challenge that the nation's second-in-command can encounter: a serious illness of the President. Eisenhower had suffered a heart attack in 1955, but he recovered fairly quickly. In 1957, though, he suffered a stroke, and his recovery was slower and less certain.

Nixon was in a delicate position. One of the primary responsibilities of the Vice-President is to take over the leadership of the government if the President dies or is unable to govern. If a President dies, the Vice-President automatically becomes President. But if a President is ill, the Vice-President's task is much more difficult. He must do what needs to be done, yet he must avoid doing too much. If he looks too eager or tries to take on too many responsibilities while the President is ill or recovering from an illness, a Vice-President may be accused of being power-hungry or heartless. Yet if he shows too much caution, he may be accused of being weak or indecisive.

Nixon rose to this crisis with great skill and sensitivity. For once, his admirers and his opponents were forced to agree. All felt that the Vice-President did a thoughtful, mature, and competent job of running the administration until Ike recovered his strength. His performance during Eisenhower's illness was one of the high points of Nixon's two terms as Vice-President.

Beyond the Borders

In terms of Nixon's lifelong political career, the most important thing that happened to him during his second term as Vice-President was that he became something of an international figure. A decade after World War II, the world now seemed to be smaller. A growing number of people recognized the importance of international relations and the idea of a community of nations. Eisenhower made Nixon America's spokesman in that community. He sent Nixon on a number of trips to visit foreign nations and meet their heads of state.

Most of these trips and meetings were purely ceremonial; that is, they were formal or official occasions at which little real diplomatic or political business took place. But these events were very visible to the whole world and gave Nixon the chance to become an international figure, not just an American one. They also gave him the chance to learn a great deal about other nations, other people, and other leaders.

On his first long trip overseas, Nixon visited 19 nations in the Far East. He then went on a tour of nine African countries. It was while he was in Ghana, which had just become an independent black republic, that he first met the Reverend Dr. Martin Luther King, Jr., a civil-rights leader from the United States. Dr. King later tried to get Vice-President Nixon's help in passing civil-rights laws in the United States, and Nixon did support the civil-rights bill that Congress passed in 1957.

A Riot in Caracas

In addition to his trips to the Orient and to Africa, Nixon made several visits to European nations. But the most important of his foreign travels were to South America and the Soviet Union. The South American tour took place in 1958, and it did not go well for the U.S. visitors. In Lima, Peru, the local Communist Party organized a protest against Nixon's visit. Hundreds of students and workers gathered outside his hotel, waving signs that read "Out Nixon!" At one point, a crowd blocked the road in front of his limousine. Against the advice of his security guards, Nixon insisted on getting out and confronting the crowd, only to be spat upon and pelted with fruit.

Worse was yet to come. In Caracas, Venezuela, a hostile mob led by local Communists greeted Nixon's arrival at the airport with signs and shaking fists. Demonstrators showered spittle on Nixon and Pat as they entered the terminal building, but, to the amazement of everyone present, the Nixons did not run for cover. Instead, they endured unbelievable humiliation and discomfort as they stood at attention while the band played the Venezuelan national anthem. Only when it was finished did they enter their limousines for the ride to their hotel. By this time, however, the crowd had grown larger and even uglier. People blocked the road and rocked Nixon's car from side to side, while others hurled rocks through the car windows. The Venezuelan military police who accompanied the limousines on motorcycles seemed unable or unwilling to take action.

Suddenly the situation was dangerous indeed. The rioters thrust wooden sticks through the broken windows. Hands appeared, grabbing at the passengers. Fearing that the Vice-President's life was in danger, Nixon's guards drew their revolvers, but he ordered them not to shoot. After five or ten agonizingly long minutes, a squad of Venezuelan soldiers arrived and cleared a path through the crowd. As soon as the cars could move, Nixon ordered them to go to the U.S. embassy. There the group stayed while anti-American crowds continued to riot through the streets of Caracas.

A Hero's Welcome

Radio reports reaching the United States raised grave fears for Nixon's safety. Eisenhower ordered a detachment of troops to be ready to advance to Caracas at a moment's notice if it became necessary to rescue the Vice-President from the embassy. It is possible that such a move could have brought war between the United States and Venezuela; certainly it would have given the anti-American elements in South America new reasons to claim that the United States was interfering in South American affairs. Fortunately, however, the Venezuelan government managed to control the disturbance, and Nixon's group was able to leave for Washington the next day.

To Nixon's delight and astonishment, he received a hero's welcome when he arrived home. All government workers had been given the afternoon off in honor of his safe return, and about 15,000 of them gathered at the airport to cheer as he and Pat stepped from the plane. Among them was Eisenhower, who warmly praised Nixon's courage.

Khrushchev in the Kitchen

Nixon became a hero of another sort on his next trip, which took place in 1959. It was a goodwill tour of the Soviet Union. One of Nixon's duties during the tour was to preside at the opening ceremonies of a display of American consumer products in Moscow. The Soviet premier, Nikita Khrushchev, also attended the opening. He and Nixon engaged in an unscheduled, informal, day-long debate as they wandered through the exhibition hall.

The conversation between the two leaders ranged from women's rights to nuclear war. Khrushchev, a short, solidly built former mine-worker, had a reputation for tough talk and for bullying. But Nixon held his own with the Soviet leader. At one point, the two men halted in a model of a modern American kitchen. Arguing the merits of capitalism over communism, Nixon went nose-to-nose with Khrushchev and poked the Soviet premier in the chest with a forefinger to drive home a point. Although Khrushchev took this highly personal form of argument in good spirit, an American news photographer captured the moment as a dramatic confrontation — between two men, two nations, and two ways of life. The picture appeared on the cover of *Time* magazine.

Along with the riot in Caracas, the "kitchen debate," as the incident with Khrushchev came to be called, showed Nixon as a bold leader who was not afraid to stand up for America around the world. This image endeared him to many voters.

At the end of eight years in office, Nixon was the most widely traveled Vice-President in U.S. history. In spite of Eisenhower's reluctance to give him any real power or role in running the government, Nixon had made himself into something of an expert on foreign affairs and international relations. Throughout the rest of his political career, in fact, his greatest successes would be at the international level. And now, as Eisenhower's presidency neared its close, Nixon was ready to get on with that career.

Chapter 7

Defeat and Victory

By 1960, Nixon had been in political life for 14 years. His daughters had grown into teenagers in Washington: Tricia into a quiet blonde who adored the rare treat of attending a baseball game with her father, and Julie into a bubbly, outgoing brunette who daydreamed of becoming an actress. Although politics had ruled Nixon's life, Pat had succeeded in providing a fairly private, unspoiled family life for the girls, even though their family vacations were usually taken without their father, and they often saw little of him for days at a time. Yet the family remained genuinely close and affectionate.

A DESIRED ENDORSEMENT

Nixon's career had lived up to his hopes. He had risen rapidly, without a single setback, from a junior congressman to the Vice-President of the United States. Now Eisenhower's two terms as President were nearly over. It seemed to Nixon — and to most of his fellow Republicans — that the logical choice for the next Republican presidential candidate was Richard M. Nixon. Unfortunately, one important Republican did not appear to share that view. This was President Eisenhower.

Nixon badly wanted Eisenhower to announce his support for Nixon before the 1960 Republican National Convention, where the party would nominate its presidential candidate. Although Nixon felt that he would win the nomination, an endorsement (or statement of support) from Eisenhower would help make it certain. In fact, Nixon knew that it would look odd if Eisenhower *did not* endorse him. It would appear that the President lacked confidence in his Vice-President.

Eisenhower's own mixed feelings about Nixon did not help matters. While Ike respected Nixon's courage and intelligence, he did not care a great deal for him personally, and he knew that Nixon disagreed with him on some basic political issues. Eisenhower would have preferred to see the nomination go to someone who shared more of his own ideas, even though Nixon was the strongest candidate. As a result, Eisenhower did little or nothing to help Nixon win the nomination.

Some of Eisenhower's remarks actually hurt Nixon. At one point, when reporters asked Eisenhower to name one of Nixon's ideas or contributions to the Eisenhower presidency, Ike snapped, "If you give me a week, I might think of one." Eisenhower later apologized to Nixon for the remark, but the damage was done, and Nixon never forgave him. When Eisenhower offered to make campaign speeches, Nixon refused.

The Republicans chose Nixon anyway, as everyone had expected them to do. They also chose Henry Cabot Lodge, a former senator from Massachusetts and representative to the United Nations, as the vice-presidential candidate. Having won the nomination, Nixon set out to win the election. His Democratic opponent was Massachusetts Senator John F. Kennedy.

THE CAMPAIGN OF 1960

Nixon and Kennedy were surprisingly alike in some ways. Both were young—Kennedy was 43, Nixon 47. Both were intelligent, ambitious men who had moved quickly up the political ladder and had broad support within their respective parties. But there were great differences, as well. Nixon was a self-made man from a humble West Coast background; Kennedy was from one of the nation's wealthiest and most prominent East Coast families. Nixon had an undistinguished war record; Kennedy was a true war hero.

Nixon had several advantages as the race began. First, he had made himself very visible as the country's international spokesman, and people remembered how well he had acted during Eisenhower's illness. Kennedy, on the other hand, did not have much experience as an administrator. Furthermore, religious prejudice was on Nixon's side. Kennedy was a Roman Catholic. No Catholic had ever been elected President, and many Americans believed that none ever would be. Some people even feared that a Catholic President would be controlled by the Pope in Rome. Nixon showed good judgment and good taste in never referring to Kennedy's religion, however, and religion did not play much part in the election after Kennedy calmly assured voters that his religion could have no influence on his decisions as President.

It was in the area of race relations where the two men differed considerably. This issue played an important part in the 1960 presidential campaign, as black Americans became increasingly aware of their political power and united behind such leaders as Martin Luther King, Jr., and Ralph Bunche. For the first time, presidential candidates had to take the organized black vote into consideration.

While Nixon had indeed supported the Civil Rights Bill of 1957, Kennedy was a more enthusiastic supporter of sweeping change to bring about racial equality. Just before the election, King was arrested in a civil-rights demonstration in Atlanta, Georgia, and sentenced to a term in a hard-labor prison. Blacks and civil-rights leaders feared that white prisoners would kill King, and they appealed to both candidates for assistance. Nixon hesitated to take action, trying to decide what course would be best for his election chances, but Kennedy acted promptly. He reassured King's wife on the phone and then used his political connections to get King released from jail on bail. Black voters lined up solidly behind Kennedy, although Nixon still held the lead in nationwide polls.

TV Troubles

The real turning point in the election was not about religion, race, or even the candidates' qualifications and experience. The real turning point came on Monday, September 26, when for the first time two presidential candidates met for a face-to-face debate on live television. Before an audience of 80 million people, Nixon lost his lead to Kennedy. He was never able to get it back.

Historians have written dozens of books about the Nixon-Kennedy debates (there were four debates in all, but the first was the most important). Almost all agree that television, which Nixon had used so well in the case of the "Checkers" speech, was his downfall in the election just eight years later.

Nixon was pale with exhaustion when he arrived at the television studio for the first debate. He had spent the afternoon before the debate in his hotel room, feverishly studying his notes. His nonstop speech-making tour had caused him to lose sleep and to lose weight. His suit and shirt fit poorly, and his face looked tired and drawn. Kennedy, on the other hand, had spent the afternoon of the debate on the roof of his hotel, working on a suntan and resting.

Ironically, Nixon had looked forward to the debate. His long series of debate championships in his younger years had made him confident that he would demolish his opponent, and his victory with the "Checkers" speech had made him believe that television was a friendly medium for him. But he did not realize how good Kennedy would look on television: handsome, tanned, well rested, poised, and confident. Nor did he realize how bad *he* would look: sweaty, tired, pale, with dark circles under his eyes and an unattractive dark shadow from his heavy beard, even though he had just shaved. Nixon appeared nervous, ill-informed, and awkward, while Kennedy appeared calm, well informed, and comfortable.

Looks alone did not win or lose the debate. But it is interesting to note that radio audiences, who heard the candidates but could not see them, felt that on the whole Nixon did better in the debate than Kennedy. Television audiences, however, felt that Kennedy performed better. Many of Nixon's supporters sent him telegrams urging him to get some rest and to start wearing TV makeup before the next debate. Lodge, Nixon's vice-presidential candidate, watched the debate in Texas. Afterward he exclaimed that Nixon had "just lost us the election!"

Lodge's dire prediction was correct. The debate seemed to have pushed popular opinion toward Kennedy's direction. After seeing how well Kennedy appeared on television, more voters expressed confidence in his ability to govern. As Nixon was later to say, "Isn't that a hell of a thing—that the fate of a great country can depend on camera angles?"

Winner and Loser

The 1960 presidential election was one of the closest in American history. Kennedy received 34,221,349 popular votes and 303 electoral votes; Nixon received 34,108,647 popular votes and 219 electoral votes. In other words, Nixon lost the popular vote by only 112,702 votes out of the more than 68 million that were cast—less than one-tenth of one percent. Although it has never been proven, some evidence suggests that the vote counts in Texas and Illinois, which swung the election to Kennedy, were fraudulent; in other words, that the election went to Kennedy through dishonest means. Herb Klein, a press assistant and friend of Nixon, says that Nixon did not insist upon a close examination of the results because he feared that the disruption this would cause would be bad for the country.

Nixon was crushed by his defeat. He had been confident of success, and now he had not only lost the election but had also caused his party to lose control of the White House. Nevertheless, he presented himself as a good loser, because he did not think his career in politics was over yet. He held a friendly press conference with Kennedy after the election and managed to joke and smile with the Democratic victor. Then, when Kennedy and his Vice-President, Lyndon B. Johnson of Texas, took office in January of 1961, Nixon moved his family back home to California after 14 years in the nation's capital.

RUNNING FOR GOVERNOR

Nixon went to work in a law firm in California. But he did not turn his back on politics. He wrote many articles on political subjects for a variety of magazines and newspapers, and he made speeches at clubs and universities around the country. He also wrote a book called *Six Crises*. It described the six most crucial events of his career: the Hiss case, the slush fund embarrassment, Eisenhower's stroke, the riot in Caracas, the "kitchen debate" with Khrushchev, and the 1960 presidential campaign. The book became a best-seller and helped to keep its author in the public eye.

Not that Nixon remained out of the public eye for long. Soon after returning to California, he decided to run for governor of the state in 1962. Some of his political advisors tried to discourage him, for two reasons. First, the Democratic governor, Edmund "Pat" Brown, would be running for re-election. He was popular and would be difficult to beat. Second, even loyal Republican voters would suspect that Nixon did not really want to be governor of California but was only planning to use the governorship as a way of staying active in politics until he could run for President again. These advisors warned Nixon that if he ran for governor and lost, he might never be able to make a comeback.

But Nixon was too restless to stay out of the political arena. Calling on the support of Republican Party leaders around the state whom he had helped in the past, he won the party nomination for governor. He then launched a campaign against Brown that was similar to the campaigns he had waged against Voorhis and Douglas. He even returned to his old red-baiting tactics, trying to smear Brown with the taint of communism. Nixon supporters circulated bumper stickers that asked, "Is Brown Pink?" One of the Nixon campaign leaflets showed a photograph of Brown bowing before Soviet Premier Khrushchev; the photograph proved to have been faked.

Brown fought back. Remembering how close Nixon came to disaster over the slush fund, he ordered his campaign workers to dig into the Nixon family's finances, looking for anything that would make Nixon look bad. During the only face-to-face debate by the candidates, Brown dropped a bombshell, announcing that Nixon's brother Donald had received a personal loan of $250,000 from Howard Hughes, a multimillionaire whose aircraft company did work for the Pentagon. The suggestion was that the loan to Donald Nixon gave Hughes some power over the former Vice-President that might have helped Hughes make money from government contracts. Nixon claimed that the loan was strictly between

Donald and Hughes and that he had nothing to do with it, but the unpleasant suggestion that he might have been bought by Hughes lingered.

A Bitter Blow

The two candidates continued to slug it out in sensational headlines and heated accusations. Both were guilty of making trumped-up charges and hysterical insults, which were gleefully reported by the newspapers. But when the voters went to the polls, they voted to keep the governor they already knew in office. Brown defeated Nixon. The vote count was close, but that could not make up for the severe humiliation Nixon felt. Just two years before he had been the nation's Vice-President; now he could not even get elected governor in his home state. It was a bitter blow, so bitter that a tired and defeated Nixon reacted with anger. At a press conference at the Beverly Hilton Hotel, he turned against the reporters.

Nixon had never cared much for reporters. He believed that most of them favored the Democrats, and like many anti-Communists of the McCarthy era, he felt that they were too soft on communism. As time went on, he began to feel that the press had singled him out for especially cruel and unfair treatment. "The press is the enemy," he told one of his assistants. That night at the Beverly Hilton, he raged at the assembled reporters "for being so delighted that I have lost." He complained that the press had been attacking him for 16 years, ever since the Hiss case, and then he added dramatically, "But as I leave you I want you to know—just think how much you're going to be missing. You won't have Nixon to kick around any more, because, gentlemen, this is my last press conference."

This angry, awkward farewell made headlines across the land. No one knew for certain whether Nixon had planned it or whether he had simply given in to a sudden impulse, but everyone agreed on one thing: Nixon would never be able to live down the "last press conference" remark. He was out of politics for good, his enemies and friends alike believed. But Nixon could not be easily forgotten. When the American Broadcasting Company ran a show called "The Political Obituary of Richard Nixon," which featured complaints about Nixon from guest Alger Hiss, more than 80,000 viewers wrote or called to tell of their support for Nixon. Perhaps some of them suspected that although Nixon might be down, he was by no means out.

A TIME OF TURMOIL

Nixon did not want to remain in California after losing the governor race. The family moved to New York City, where the former Vice-President went to work for a large law firm. Tricia and Julie were enrolled in a private school. Nixon, however, continued to write political articles, to make speeches, and to maintain his position as a leader in the Republican Party.

The 1960s were a time of great turmoil in the United States. President Kennedy was assassinated in 1963, and his successor, Lyndon B. Johnson, plunged the country deeper and deeper into war in Vietnam, an obscure country in southeast Asia where U.S. troops were fighting to keep South Vietnam from being invaded by Communist forces from North Vietnam. At the same time, taxes went up, cities such as Detroit and Los Angeles erupted in violent race riots, and the Democratic Party slowly began to lose its hold on political power in Washington.

By the end of the 1960s, opposition to U.S. participation in the Vietnam War was on the rise. Here, antiwar demonstrators march toward Capitol Hill in 1971. (Copyright *Washington Post;* reprinted by permission of the D.C. Public Library.)

Some people thought that the Republicans had a chance to win the presidency in 1964. Barry Goldwater was the Republican candidate, and Nixon lent his wholehearted support to Goldwater's campaign, once again playing the part of the loyal and hardworking party soldier. He traveled 50,000 miles to make speeches in 36 states during the campaign. Goldwater lost by a landslide – but party leaders and voters were reminded of Nixon's faithful service.

As the Vietnam War increased in size and violence during the later 1960s, opposition to the war increased on college campuses at home. By 1967 there were more than 400,000 American servicemen fighting in Vietnam. But many Americans, especially young people, felt that the United States was wrong to interfere in Vietnam's affairs by sending troops to South Vietnam and bombing cities in North Vietnam. President Johnson was growing increasingly unpopular with the American people for his inability to end the war in Vietnam and for the failure of his ambitious programs to aid the poor. Early in 1968, he announced that he would not run for re-election that year.

THE WHITE HOUSE AT LAST

A number of Democrats competed for their party's nomination. Robert Kennedy, brother of the assassinated President, might have been nominated, but he, too, was tragically assassinated during his campaign. Eventually the nomination went to Hubert Humphrey, who had served as Johnson's Vice-President. A third party, the American Independent Party, sponsored its own candidate, former Governor George Wallace of Alabama. It was generally agreed that Wallace had no chance to win.

In the meantime, Nixon quietly and steadily gathered support among the Republicans. His six-year withdrawal from political life actually helped him, because it placed him in a neutral position, unlike the other Republican candidates, who had been fighting among themselves during the Democratic administration. When the Republican National Convention met in Miami Beach in August of 1968, Nixon was their first choice. He selected Spiro Agnew, the governor of Maryland, as his vice-presidential candidate. In his speech accepting the nomination, Nixon said, "Let us begin by committing ourselves to the truth—to see it like it is, and tell it like it is—to find the truth, to speak the truth, and to live the truth." Half a dozen years later, amid the lies of Watergate, this pledge was remembered with scorn.

A "New Nixon"

The 1968 presidential campaign introduced America to what Nixon's supporters said was really a "new Nixon." He was more relaxed and less angry than the Nixon whom many remembered. He appeared to have abandoned the campaign tactics that had worked against Voorhis and Douglas but had failed against Brown. Instead of attacking Humphrey personally, Nixon attacked the Democrats for causing the country's problems. Because he made far fewer speeches and public appearances than in previous campaigns, the press and the public did not have many chances to catch him off guard or provoke a hostile response. Nixon's entire approach was careful and reasonable.

This cautious approach worked. More than 32,000 Americans had died in Vietnam. Many voters were tired of the conflict in Southeast Asia and also of the antiwar protest movement that seemed to be tearing American society apart. These voters longed for a return to the simple, law-and-order atmosphere of the 1950s. Nixon seemed to offer this. He also promised that he had "a secret plan" to end the war; he could not give details, he said, because they might interfere with the peace talks then going on in Paris between the United States and South and North Vietnam. The nation was hungry for such reassurances. Despite a rise in Humphrey's popularity just before election day, Nixon won the election.

Nixon had hoped for a landslide win to prove his popularity, but the vote count was extremely close. Nonetheless, he had finally achieved a lifelong goal. The humiliation of his losses in 1960 and 1962 was swallowed up in the glorious fact that on election day in 1968, Richard M. Nixon was the 37th President of the United States.

Chapter **8**

The Nixon Presidency

Nixon was sworn in as President on January 20, 1969. His daughter Tricia was there. So was Julie, accompanied by her new husband (she had married Dwight David Eisenhower, grandson of the former President, one month earlier). Pat Nixon held the Bible for her husband's swearing-in. She wore a "respectable Republican cloth coat," like the one Nixon had described those many years ago in the "Checkers" speech—but this time she also wore a fur hat.

DOMESTIC AFFAIRS

By the time Nixon became President, the American public had become split into many groups, each opposing the others and each demanding that certain things be done. Among these groups were protestors against the Vietnam War, blacks seeking civil rights, and workers worried about unemployment and the high cost of living. In his inaugural speech, Nixon

A White House portrait taken in front of a painting of George Washington shows the Nixons with son-in-law David Eisenhower (left), daughter Julie (seated left), daughter Tricia (seated right), and son-in-law Edward Cox (right). (Nixon Project, National Archives.)

spoke of bringing everyone together, but he really wanted the support of what he called "the silent majority," the huge population of middle-class Americans who were tired of crime, street riots, and confusing changes in society's values.

Young people were pleased when Nixon's administration passed the 26th Amendment to the Constitution in 1971, lowering the voting age from 21 to 18 years. But many of these new voters opposed Nixon's leadership and promised to vote against him in 1972.

School Desegregation

In the area of civil rights, the issue of the day was school desegregation—that is, switching from a system of separate schools for black and white students to a system in which black and white students would attend the same schools. In 1969, the Supreme Court ordered that desegregation was necessary to ensure equal rights to blacks. The question was how to accomplish it. Another Supreme Court decision upheld "busing," or carrying students from all-white or all-black communities to mixed schools in school buses, as a way of achieving desegregation.

Busing was far from universally popular, however; many people in both the North and the South felt that it was expensive, time-consuming, and not likely to improve anyone's education. Nixon spoke out publicly against busing, and he ordered it kept to the minimum required by law. Civil-rights activists claimed that his policies slowed the process of achieving equal rights. However, although Nixon is not generally regarded as being supportive of civil rights, the civil-rights movement made great strides forward during his administration.

Economic Woes

Economic problems also plagued the Nixon administration. Unemployment was on the rise; the cost of consumer goods and housing kept going up; and inflation also rose rapidly—

in other words, the purchasing power of the dollar was falling. Nixon reduced government spending on many social programs that had been started under Johnson, such as the Job Corps (a training and employment service for low-income youth) and school lunches paid for by the federal government.

Under Nixon, millions of tax dollars were returned from the federal government to the state and local governments. This program, called revenue sharing, was intended to make local governments take responsibility for those programs and services that were no longer being paid for by the federal government. Critics complained, however, that it would have been fairer and more efficient to continue the federal programs, because not all the states replaced them.

Domestic Achievements

Nixon's first term in office did see some achievements in domestic affairs. Growing concern over pollution and damage to the environment led to the establishment of the Environmental Protection Agency (EPA), a federal organization to administer antipollution laws. The Nixon administration passed several acts aimed at cleaning up the nation's air and waterways. Nixon also pushed several bills through Congress that strengthened law enforcement against organized crime and against suspected drug dealers.

One of the most exciting achievements of the Nixon years came in July of 1969, when astronauts Neil Armstrong and Edwin Aldrin became the first people to walk on the surface of the moon. Millions of people watched their television sets in awe as the space travelers, clad in bulky silver suits, bounded across what Aldrin described as the "magnificent desolation" of the earth's only satellite. In a telephone call

Men on the Moon

Although the first moon landing took place during Nixon's presidency, the U.S. space program really got its start under President Eisenhower, who was upset because the Russians, not the Americans, launched the first space satellite. Under Eisenhower and then Presidents Kennedy and Johnson, the National Aeronautics and Space Administration (NASA) pushed America's frontiers outward into space, first with robot satellites, then with manned flights and earth orbits, and finally with the Apollo 11 mission that put men on the moon for the first time.

The Apollo 11 spacecraft, called the *Columbia,* lifted off from Florida on July 16, 1969, watched by a million spectators at the launch site and millions more on television. Three days later, the spacecraft went into orbit around the moon. Astronauts Neil Armstrong and Edwin Aldrin then entered a smaller vehicle, called the *Eagle,* for the actual landing on the lunar surface. The two men piloted the *Eagle* toward a touchdown spot in a flat plain called the "Sea of Tranquility." America and the world listened to the radio broadcast from the lunar lander as it settled toward the moon's surface. Then Armstrong's voice broke the tension. "Tranquility Base here," he said. "The *Eagle* has landed."

A few hours later, a door opened in the side of the *Eagle* and the heavily booted feet of Armstrong descended a ladder. As the first human visitor stepped onto the moon, he remarked to the listening audience, "That's one small step for a man, one giant leap for mankind."

The astronauts gathered rock and dust samples and took many photographs. They also planted a U.S. flag and left a plaque signed by President Nixon that said, "Here men from the planet earth first set foot upon the moon, July 1969, A.D. We came in peace for all mankind." The following day the *Eagle* lifted off the moon to rejoin the *Columbia.*

Like Columbus before them, the Apollo 11 astronauts had crossed an unknown sea to set foot upon a new world.

relayed to the astronauts' craft by radio, President Nixon told them, "Because of what you have done, the heavens have become part of man's world." However, some Americans criticized the space program, saying that the money spent to launch men into space would be better spent solving problems on earth. Yet the American moon landing remains an awe-inspiring feat, achieved after much hard work and the creation of ingenious scientific technology.

THE VIETNAM WAR

The war in Vietnam was the biggest issue of Nixon's first term as President. From his point of view, it was a war that he was forced to fight on two fronts: one in the jungles of Southeast Asia and the other on the streets and campuses of the United States.

Opposition to the war had grown steadily during Lyndon Johnson's presidency, especially among the young and those in the nation's colleges. Antiwar marches and demonstrations by shouting, sign-waving protestors occurred almost every day. From the protestors' point of view, the United States had no business fighting a war in Vietnam in the first place, and they wanted Nixon to withdraw all U.S. troops at once. They argued that it would be impossible to keep the Communists in North Vietnam from eventually overrunning South Vietnam unless the United States kept up military occupation forever.

Nixon was determined, however, not to withdraw until North Vietnam signed a treaty not to invade South Vietnam. It seemed as much a matter of personal pride as of international politics. "I'm not going to be the first American President who lost a war," he grimly vowed to an assistant.

A Plan to End the War

During his 1968 presidential campaign, Nixon had promised to end the war, but his "secret plan" was slow to get results. It consisted of bombing attacks on North Vietnam, combined with new negotiations in Paris. He also planned to withdraw American troops and replace them with trained South Vietnamese troops, a process he called "Vietnamization."

It was another aspect of Nixon's war plan, however, that disturbed many Americans. He authorized U.S. planes to drop bombs on Cambodia and Laos, two of Vietnam's neighbors who had not entered the war. These attacks were supposed to destroy hidden Communist bases that supported the North Vietnamese.

Like the bombings of North Vietnam, however, the attacks on Cambodia and Laos killed thousands of innocent civilians. They also sparked a wave of violent antiwar protests by Americans who were outraged that their President would order armed aggression against two neutral nations. When it was learned that the bombing of Cambodia had been going on for some time and that Nixon and the Defense Department had deceived Congress and the public about it, many members of the so-called "silent majority" suddenly became critics of the war.

Bloodshed at Kent State

The clash between the antiwar movement and the forces of law and order that supported government policy came to bloodshed in the spring of 1970. Ohio National Guardsmen, under orders to break up an antiwar protest, fired guns into a crowd at Kent State University and killed four students. Two weeks later, two students were killed by police gunfire at a college in Jackson, Michigan. In response to these shocking events, the antiwar movement gained strength. A protest rally in Washington in April of 1971 was one of the biggest riots the capital had ever seen.

The Pentagon Papers

A few months later, *The New York Times* began publishing a series of documents that came to be called the Pentagon Papers. They had been given to the newspaper by Daniel Ellsberg, a former official in the Defense Department. The papers showed that Presidents Kennedy and Johnson had systematically deceived the American people about what was happening in Vietnam. Nixon tried to stop publication of the papers, but the courts prevented him from doing so. Although Nixon was not included in the Pentagon Papers, they made the presidency itself appear less trustworthy and turned many more people against the war.

At this time, Nixon's distrust of anyone who did not agree with him began to shape his actions. In Nixon's view of things, anyone who did not support him was an enemy—there was no room for honest, constructive disagreement. As he had done for most of his political career, he began to lash out against those who did not share his opinions.

In addition, fearful of more "leaks" like Ellsberg's, a group of Nixon's assistants (later called the "White House plumbers" because their job was to prevent leaks) illegally tapped the phones of newspaper reporters and congressmen who were opposed to Nixon. The "plumbers" also broke into the office of Ellsberg's psychiatrist, hoping to find information in his files that would make Ellsberg look bad to the public. In short, it appeared that Nixon saw himself as being besieged by attackers and thought he could do anything he wanted in order to protect himself.

"Peace with Honor"

All the while, Nixon's Vietnamization program was under way, and the number of U.S. troops in Vietnam steadily dwindled, although bombing of North Vietnam's cities was kept up. Nixon relied on his national security advisor, Henry Kissinger, to arrive at a treaty with North Vietnam that would allow the United States to end the war without abandoning South Vietnam to the Communists. The expression that Nixon liked was "peace with honor."

In August of 1972, during Nixon's campaign for re-election, the last U.S. ground troops came home from Vietnam. The end of the war came in January of 1973, when a peace agreement was signed in Paris. The agreement called for a neutral zone to be established between North and South Vietnam. This allowed the United States to end its involvement in the war after more than 48,000 soldiers were killed in action, 304,000 were wounded, and $110 billion was spent in war expenses.

Many believed that the Americans who died had died in vain, because the Communists would sweep down from the north before the ink was dry on the peace treaty—which is just what happened. Fighting between North and South Vietnam resumed at once, and the Communists succeeded in taking over all of Vietnam by April of 1975. By that time, Nixon was no longer President.

Chapter 9

Watergate and the Cover-Up

I n spite of the opposition that he faced from antiwar groups during the first term of his presidency, Nixon was re-elected in 1972. By that time it was clear that the war was almost over, so the antiwar movement lost much of its urgency. Relieved that the nightmare in Asia was ending, many Americans were willing to give Nixon the credit.

Nixon was also helped by the fact that the Democratic presidential candidate, George McGovern, did not have strong backing from all parts of his party. Some traditional Democratic groups, such as labor unions, felt that McGovern was too intellectual, too much in favor of controversial ideas such as abortion rights and forgiveness for draft evaders—young men who had fled the country to avoid being sent to Vietnam to fight. By not backing McGovern, these Democrats strengthened Nixon's position.

INTERNATIONAL ACHIEVEMENTS

Nixon also won many votes because of two impressive achievements in foreign relations. Ever since his days as the world-traveling Vice-President, his greatest strength and interest had been in the area of international affairs. In 1972, with re-election on the horizon, he reached a new high point as an international leader because of historic visits to the People's Republic of China and the Soviet Union.

China and Russia

Nixon's achievements in foreign policy reflected a new attitude toward international communism, an attitude which he shared with the practical Kissinger. Nixon was increasingly aware that the Communist nations of the world were not one big entity but instead were many independent countries, often at odds with one another. He also realized that the United States needed to establish an individual relationship with each of these nations, including the People's Republic of China, the world's most populous nation. No U.S. diplomat had entered China since the Communists took over the country in 1949, and no American President had ever gone there.

In February 1972 Nixon became the first U.S. President to go to China. It was a momentous occasion. Between visits to sights such as the Great Wall, Nixon and Chinese leader Mao Tse-Tung signed a number of agreements that opened the way for trade and political relations between the two nations.

Nixon's China trip ended more than two decades of ignorance and hostility between China and the United States. It also paved the way for China to enter the world community. His trip to China is generally regarded as the highest achievement of Nixon's political career.

Another high point came just three months later, when Nixon visited the Soviet Union. There he and Soviet Premier Leonid Brezhnev signed a treaty that they hoped would limit

Nixon's trip to China was a historic meeting of cultures. In addition to conversations with Mao Tse-Tung, the chairman of China's Communist Party, Nixon shared a traditional Chinese meal with Premier Chou En-Lai in Shanghai. (Nixon Project, National Archives.)

the development of nuclear weapons in both the United States and the Soviet Union. People around the world greeted the summit meeting of the two leaders (called Strategic Arms Limitation Talks, or SALT) as a step on the road to world peace.

*Soviet Premier Leonid Brezhnev and Nixon sign an arms treaty.
Nixon's excellent handling of U.S. relations with the Soviet
Union and China was his most impressive accomplishment as
President.* (Nixon Project, National Archives.)

SECOND-TERM TROUBLES

Buoyed by these triumphs, Nixon won re-election in 1972 by
a substantial majority. But just as his first term was dominated by the Vietnam War, his second term was overshadowed
by one of the most disturbing episodes in the history of American politics: the Watergate affair.

The Break-in at Watergate

The Watergate affair has been called "the dark side of Nixon's
presidency." While historical analysts are still examining this
scandalous episode, some believe that it may have come about
because of certain elements in Nixon's character. One of these
characteristics was his apparent scorn and fear of people who

did not agree with him. Another was his belief that, as President, he could take whatever action he thought necessary to protect himself from his "enemies," even if his actions broke the law. In fact, at one point, Nixon actually said, "When the President does it, that means it is not illegal."

The Watergate break-in was planned at a 1972 meeting of a group of Nixon's supporters who called themselves the Committee to Re-Elect the President. A number of these committee members conspired to use illegal campaign funds to place hidden listening devices in the Democratic headquarters. Among the conspirators were G. Gordon Liddy, a former FBI agent, and E. Howard Hunt, a former CIA agent.

The Cover-Up Attempt

Even more damaging to Nixon than the break-in itself was the attempted cover-up, which began at once. Investigators would later learn that Nixon authorized the payment of at least $400,000 from his campaign fund to the five men who had been arrested at the Watergate building so that they would keep his name out of the matter. He ordered all of his assistants and the members of the re-election committee to deny all knowledge of the break-in.

The cover-up worked at first. Watergate did not play much of a role in the 1972 presidential election, and most people still believed that the President was innocent of a cover-up attempt. He told the American public that John Dean, who held the post of lawyer to the President, had investigated the charges of a cover-up and proved that no cover-up existed. But in 1973, during his burglary trial, one of the five men who had been arrested for his part in the break-in claimed that he had been bribed to lie for the President. This shocking news caused people to sit up and take notice, and the Senate set up a committee to find out the truth.

The Cover-Up Springs Leaks

Throughout 1973 gaping holes were torn in Nixon's cover-up efforts. Some of his closest advisors—Liddy and Hunt as well as John Ehrlichman and H.R. Haldeman—admitted that they had known about the break-in. They were charged with perjury (lying under oath in a court of law) because they had already sworn that they knew nothing about it. Most dramatic of all was the Senate testimony of Nixon's lawyer, John Dean, who finally broke down and admitted on television that the President had been aware of the cover-up from the beginning.

After this bombshell, Nixon could not move quickly enough to plug all the information leaks in his administration. Investigators uncovered one disturbing fact after another. Dean testified that Nixon kept a secret "enemies" list of news reporters, people in government, and popular entertainers whom he felt were "out to get him." The President had ordered the phones of some of these individuals to be illegally tapped by the FBI and had encouraged the Internal Revenue Service to make life difficult for his "enemies" by auditing their tax returns. Unfortunately for Nixon, this prompted an investigation into his own finances, and it turned out that he owed the government more than $450,000 in unpaid taxes.

Trouble with Agnew

In the summer of 1973, in the middle of the Watergate troubles, Nixon faced a new crisis. Spiro Agnew, his Vice-President, was charged with a number of crimes. Some of

The testimony of John Dean, Nixon's lawyer, blew the Watergate cover-up wide open and effectively ended Nixon's presidency. Dean admitted on television that Nixon had authorized the cover-up and had deceived the public from the start of the Watergate affair. (Copyright *Washington Post*; reprinted by permission of the D.C. Public Library.)

Gerald Ford (right), a Republican congressman from Michigan, was Nixon's choice to succeed disgraced Spiro Agnew as Vice-President. (Nixon Project, National Archives.)

these crimes involved illegal payments that had been made to Agnew while he was an official in Maryland, and some involved bribes that he had received as Vice-President. Agnew agreed to resign from the vice-presidency. He did not stand trial on the charges against him, but he was fined $10,000 and put on probation for three years. The Agnew affair was another enormous black mark on the Nixon presidency, even though none of the charges against Agnew concerned Watergate.

To replace Agnew as Vice-President, Nixon selected

Gerald Ford, a well-liked Republican congressman from Michigan. Ford had a reputation for honesty and was not connected with Watergate or any other scandals of the Nixon administration.

The Oval Office Tapes

In a way, Nixon brought about his own final downfall. He used a secret tape-recording system in the White House to keep records of everything that he and his advisors said—he claimed that he planned to use the tapes to write his memoirs after he retired. (Other Presidents, notably Kennedy and Johnson, had also secretly recorded meetings.) But when the Senate committee that was investigating Watergate learned of the existence of the tapes, Nixon was doomed.

The President and the Senate fought for more than a year over the tapes. Nixon claimed that they were his property; the Senate claimed that they were evidence. Finally, the Supreme Court ordered Nixon to surrender the tapes. They clearly revealed that Nixon had known about the cover-up and had encouraged it.

One tape had a mysterious gap of 18½ minutes at a crucial point where the President's guilt was being discussed. Technical experts said that it had been erased. Rose Mary Woods, Nixon's loyal secretary, claimed that she had accidentally pushed the "erase" button while answering the telephone.

As soon as the tapes became public, Nixon's guilt was established beyond doubt. Many members of the public and of Congress had been calling for his impeachment. If impeached, Nixon would stand trial before the Senate; if found guilty, he would be thrown out of office. After hearing evidence of Nixon's guilt and deception in his own voice on the tapes, the House of Representatives recommended impeachment on July 27, 1974.

Knowing that he could not win, Nixon decided to resign. He left office the following week, and Gerald Ford became the new President of the United States. One of Ford's first acts as President was to issue "a full, free, and absolute pardon" for any and all crimes that Nixon might have committed while in office. This meant that although 30 of Nixon's assistants and advisors went to jail for their part in the Watergate affair, Nixon never stood trial. While some have criticized Ford's pardon of Nixon, others feel that it was a wise step toward quickly healing this crisis in the nation's history.

Chapter **10**

Restless Retirement

After Nixon's resignation on August 9, 1974, he and Pat withdrew to their home in San Clemente, California. There Nixon set to work writing his life story, for which he received a $2.5-million advance from a New York publisher. The book, entitled *RN: The Memoirs of Richard Nixon,* was published in two volumes in 1977 and 1979.

Nixon also was paid $600,000 for the only television interview about Watergate that he has ever given. It took place in 1977. In one of his few public remarks about the scandal that ended his presidency, Nixon told interviewer David Frost, "I let down my friends, I let down the country. . . . I let the American people down. And I have to carry that burden with me for the rest of my life. My political life is over."

A NEW ROLE

It certainly seemed that Nixon's political life was over. No American President had ever left office under a darker cloud of scorn and shame than Richard M. Nixon. But in the solitude of San Clemente, he said to friends, "I don't intend to just fade away."

Gradually, Nixon began to see the possibility of a new role for himself—not "political life" but "public life." He decided to move away from the West Coast, closer to the seat of government. He also wanted to be closer to his daughters and their families. Julie and David Eisenhower had settled in Chester County, Pennsylvania. Tricia and her husband, Edward Cox, whom she had married in a White House ceremony in 1971, lived in New York City. In 1980 Nixon and Pat also moved to New York. A year later they settled in a large house in Upper Saddle River, New Jersey. And over the decade that followed Watergate, Nixon slowly emerged as something of a spokesman, especially on international affairs.

This process started with his books. In addition to his memoirs, Nixon published *The Real War* (1980), *Leaders* (1982), *Real Peace* (1983), and *No More Vietnams* (1985). In these books he gave his own accounts of what he had accomplished as President as well as his views and opinions about world affairs in general. He also began to make cautious public appearances. The first such appearance was a speech at a Republican fund-raiser in Columbus, Ohio, in 1981. When Nixon stepped onto the platform, the crowd gave him a standing ovation. To some Republicans, it seemed, Nixon was still much loved.

Later that same year, at the request of President Ronald Reagan, Nixon accompanied former Presidents Gerald Ford and Jimmy Carter to the funeral of assassinated Egyptian President Anwar Sadat. It was clear to all that Nixon was an official representative of the United States at the funeral. Since that time, he has met unofficially to discuss international affairs with world leaders in the Mideast and the Soviet Union (a trip to Moscow in 1986 was his sixth). He has

Former Presidents Gerald Ford (left), Jimmy Carter (right center), and Nixon meet with President Ronald Reagan (left center) before attending the funeral of Egyptian President Anwar Sadat in 1981. Since then, Nixon has occasionally acted as an unofficial political advisor, drawing upon his vast knowledge of international affairs. He vowed not to let his resignation end his public life. (Nixon Project, National Archives.)

also shared his knowledge of world affairs with subsequent Presidents and other American leaders, and he has even given unofficial political advice to party leaders and government figures on occasion. Although he is aging and suffers from phlebitis (a disease of the veins), it is clear that Nixon has not just faded away.

THE MAN AND THE PRESIDENT

No political leader in U.S. history has been as controversial as Richard M. Nixon. In the face of the intense emotions that surrounded his political acts and especially his presidency, it has been difficult for historians and scholars to arrive at a true understanding of Nixon and the Nixon years. Yet most of them agree that Nixon was a man of undeniable intelligence whose very real achievements were tragically overshadowed by a scandal that he brought upon himself.

Successes and Failures

Nixon's greatest contributions as President were in the field of foreign policy. By the time he was elected President, the United States had been involved in the Vietnam War for more than a decade. Nixon did manage to end that involvement, although not as quickly or as cleanly as many people would have liked.

With the help of Henry Kissinger, Nixon also opened relations with China and improved relations with the Soviet Union. He also worked toward a cease-fire in the constant warfare between Arabs and Israelis in the Middle East, a task that would be carried on by Gerald Ford and Jimmy Carter.

Against this impressive record is the fact that Nixon made little progress in domestic issues, such as civil rights and the economy. And the real tragedy of Watergate is that it need not have happened at all.

Some writers, in an attempt to psychoanalyze Nixon, have suggested that a lifelong sense of insecurity and a fear of not being quite good enough can be traced back to Nixon's early experiences. These observers feel that his insecurities made Nixon power-hungry, suspicious, and overly eager to attack others.

But whatever the psychological reasons behind them may be, Nixon's actions must finally stand on their own. And the reality of those actions is that he did not live up to the American presidency; he disgraced it. His own words are probably the best summary of Nixon's failure: "I let the American people down. And I have to carry that burden with me for the rest of my life."

Bibliography

Ambrose, Steven. *Nixon: Volume 1—The Education of a President, 1913–1962*. New York: Simon & Schuster, 1987. This first volume in a planned multi-volume Nixon biography is lengthy, but it is the single best and most authoritative source of information about the first half-century of Nixon's life.

Anson, Robert Sam. *Exile: The Unquiet Oblivion of Richard M. Nixon*. New York: Simon & Schuster, 1984. This book describes Nixon's personal and political activities in the decade after he resigned from the presidency.

Brodie, Fawn. *Nixon: The Shaping of His Character*. New York: W.W. Norton, 1981. The author examines Nixon's family background, education, military career, and early years in law and politics. Her special interest is in showing psychological patterns that developed throughout Nixon's life and caused the tragedy of his presidency.

Ehrlichman, John. *Witness to Power: The Nixon Years*. New York: Simon & Schuster, 1982. Many of Nixon's associates have written books about him, but this is one of the most interesting. It is an inside story of the Nixon presidency and of Watergate, by one of the chief participants in the cover-up.

The End of a Presidency, by the staff of the *New York Times,* New York: Holt, Rinehart, and Winston, 1974; and *The Fall of the President,* by the staff of the *Washington Post,* New York: Dell, 1974. Two collections of essays and articles by reporters for two of the nation's top newspapers present a variety of viewpoints on

Nixon's character, his career, and Watergate. These pieces are of special interest because they were written close to the events they describe, and they capture the strong emotions and powerful national anxieties of the time.

Kissinger, Henry. *Years of Upheaval.* Boston: Little, Brown, 1982. Nixon's best legacy was his shrewd and determined management of foreign affairs. In this book, his principal advisor on international relations describes Nixon's enormous influence on world affairs from 1969 until after he left the White House.

Levitt, Morton and Micheal. *A Tissue of Lies: Nixon vs. Hiss.* New York: McGraw-Hill, 1979. The authors present a detailed account of the still-unresolved spy case that made Nixon famous.

McGinniss, Joe. *The Selling of the President, 1968.* New York: Pocket Books, 1970. This account of Nixon's victory over Hubert Humphrey focuses on the use of television and other campaign strategies.

Nixon, Richard M. *RN: The Memoirs of Richard Nixon.* New York: Grosset & Dunlap, Volume 1, 1977; Volume 2, 1979. Nixon's own story contains very little of what readers might hope for: inside information about his deepest feelings and about Watergate. But it does contain interesting and revealing material about the man and his political struggles.

Nixon, Richard M. *Six Crises.* New York: Doubleday, 1962. This book was Nixon's first. It is his account of what he thought were the six most important events of his early political career: the Hiss case, the Checkers speech, Eisenhower's heart attack, the mob violence in Caracas, the confrontation with Khrushchev in the Soviet Union, and the 1960 campaign against John F. Kennedy.

Safire, William. *Before the Fall: An Inside View of the Pre-Watergate White House.* Garden City, New York: Doubleday, 1975.

One of Nixon's speechwriters gives a revealing, sometimes amusing, look at life and politics inside the White House before things fell apart.

White, Theodore H. *Breach of Faith*. New York: Dell, 1975. The same author who wrote about Nixon's last election in 1972 produced this detailed study of his fall from power. Nixon's lifelong political history is discussed, but the emphasis is on a day-by-day, almost hour-by-hour, account of Watergate, the cover-up, and Nixon's decision to resign from office.

White, Theodore H. *The Making of the President, 1972*. New York: Atheneum, 1973. A respected journalist surveys Nixon's triumphant 1972 campaign against George McGovern. He examines the roles played by television, newspapers, and advertising, as well as by the candidates' political advisors.

Woodward, Bob, and Bernstein, Carl. *All the President's Men*. New York: Simon & Schuster, 1974. This book, which was made into a successful movie, gives the story of Watergate and the cover-up from the point of view of the two *Washington Post* reporters who brought the story to the nation's attention.

Index

PRESIDENTS OF THE UNITED STATES

GEORGE WASHINGTON	L. Falkof	0-944483-19-4
JOHN ADAMS	R. Stefoff	0-944483-10-0
THOMAS JEFFERSON	R. Stefoff	0-944483-07-0
JAMES MADISON	B. Polikoff	0-944483-22-4
JAMES MONROE	R. Stefoff	0-944483-11-9
JOHN QUINCY ADAMS	M. Greenblatt	0-944483-21-6
ANDREW JACKSON	R. Stefoff	0-944483-08-9
MARTIN VAN BUREN	R. Ellis	0-944483-12-7
WILLIAM HENRY HARRISON	R. Stefoff	0-944483-54-2
JOHN TYLER	L. Falkof	0-944483-60-7
JAMES K. POLK	M. Greenblatt	0-944483-04-6
ZACHARY TAYLOR	D. Collins	0-944483-17-8
MILLARD FILLMORE	K. Law	0-944483-61-5
FRANKLIN PIERCE	F. Brown	0-944483-25-9
JAMES BUCHANAN	D. Collins	0-944483-62-3
ABRAHAM LINCOLN	R. Stefoff	0-944483-14-3
ANDREW JOHNSON	R. Stevens	0-944483-16-X
ULYSSES S. GRANT	L. Falkof	0-944483-02-X
RUTHERFORD B. HAYES	N. Robbins	0-944483-23-2
JAMES A. GARFIELD	F. Brown	0-944483-63-1
CHESTER A. ARTHUR	R. Stevens	0-944483-05-4
GROVER CLEVELAND	D. Collins	0-944483-01-1
BENJAMIN HARRISON	R. Stevens	0-944483-15-1
WILLIAM McKINLEY	D. Collins	0-944483-55-0
THEODORE ROOSEVELT	R. Stefoff	0-944483-09-7
WILLIAM H. TAFT	L. Falkof	0-944483-56-9
WOODROW WILSON	D. Collins	0-944483-18-6
WARREN G. HARDING	A. Canadeo	0-944483-64-X
CALVIN COOLIDGE	R. Stevens	0-944483-57-7

HERBERT C. HOOVER	B. Polikoff	0-944483-58-5
FRANKLIN D. ROOSEVELT	M. Greenblatt	0-944483-06-2
HARRY S. TRUMAN	D. Collins	0-944483-00-3
DWIGHT D. EISENHOWER	R. Ellis	0-944483-13-5
JOHN F. KENNEDY	L. Falkof	0-944483-03-8
LYNDON B. JOHNSON	L. Falkof	0-944483-20-8
RICHARD M. NIXON	R. Stefoff	0-944483-59-3
GERALD R. FORD	D. Collins	0-944483-65-8
JAMES E. CARTER	D. Richman	0-944483-24-0
RONALD W. REAGAN	N. Robbins	0-944483-66-6
GEORGE H.W. BUSH	R. Stefoff	0-944483-67-4

GARRETT EDUCATIONAL CORPORATION
130 EAST 13TH STREET
ADA, OK 74820